The Collector's Encyclopedia Of
NIPPON PORCELAIN

by Joan F. Van Patten

COLLECTOR BOOKS

A Division of Schroeder Publishing Co., Inc.

P.O. BOX 3009 • PADUCAH, KENTUCKY 42001

Dedicated to
my husband, Bob

Additional copies of this book may be ordered from:

COLLECTOR BOOKS
P.O. Box 3009
Paducah, Kentucky 42001

@$19.95 Add $.50 postage for the first book &
$.20 for each additional book.

Copyright: Joan F. Van Patten, Bill Schroeder, 1979
ISBN: 0-89145-108-0

Printed by PURCHASE PRINTERS, Paducah, Kentucky

TABLE OF CONTENTS

ACKNOWLEDGEMENTS

Woodrow Wilson once said "I use not only all the brains I have, but all I can borrow." I too have borrowed ideas, thoughts and items to be photographed from many people. Their enthusiasm and encouragement has made this book such an exciting and worthwhile event for me. To all of them I give my wholehearted thanks and sincere appreciation.

First, I want to thank BILL SCHROEDER, Publisher, for giving me the opportunity to do this book. He has been extremely patient and understanding with all the problems encountered. I was allowed great flexibility as to how the book should be set up and without his help and backing none of this would have been possible.

FRANK BERNING, Photographer, has spent countless hours photographing these items. He has an artistic flair for arranging items and the pictures speak for themselves, I couldn't be more pleased.

To my friend, MADELINE FOUNTAIN, who drew all the identifying marks, I say thank you. She has also allowed me to photograph her Nippon marked Azalea pattern items for which I am grateful.

So many people helped with the book! Friends and relatives loaned their beautiful Nippon items to be photographed. My mother and father, FANNIE and ALBERT YOUNG boxed up several of their favorite items and let me bring them home so they could be added to the book. My brother, MICHAEL YOUNG, is also addicted to Nippon and many of his items can be seen in the following pages. Not only did I have my family helping but good friends as well. MARIE BUSH made weekly trips back and forth from her home wrapping and rewrapping her wares. There were times when I thought the boxes would never stop. We were always fearful that something would get broken but were very fortunate that an accident didn't occur.

JEAN COLE made several trips from Cobleskill with some of her most valuable pieces. There are approximately 50 of her prize items shown. Just one accident and several hundred dollars would have been lost. She also spent many hours with me working on the price guide for which I am grateful.

And RITA GILLIS from Syosset, N.Y., allowed us to come into her home and photograph her fantastic humidor collection and many of the other choice items you see in this book. We took pictures of over 150 pieces and she also spent hours reading the book draft for me and gave many suggestions. Without the help of all these wonderful people the book would be missing so many beautiful items. Thanks to all of you from the bottom of my heart.

Along the way one of the obstacles we encountered was how to display the dishes. Thanks go to ROBERT VAN PATTEN, JR. for building the display unit used in the book.

I also wish to thank BOB PIERCE from Kennebunk, Me. for all his advice and encouragement throughout this whole project. He always had such complete confidence and faith.

To SANDRA ANDACHT, Author, and KYLE HUSFLOEN, Editor of the *Antique Trader* who graciously allowed me to use their articles I say thank you.

To Congressman NED PATTISON and his aide CAROL GUTHERMUTH who cut through so much red tape to get the US Customs rulings for me, a special thanks.

To all the others I have corresponded with, to those who have sent copies of marks and information, thank you.

Countless hours were spent in the library, talking with dealers and collectors, going over information, deciding on photo layouts, etc. At times I wondered if it would ever get finished but I believe I can speak for myself and everyone connected with the project and say that it was truly a labor of love.

INTRODUCTION

"A thing of beauty is a joy for ever: Its loveliness increases; it will never pass into nothingness."
John Keats

The Nippon porcelain that we treasure today, that we hold in our hands and admire, how was it made? Who was it that designed and ornamented these items? Such workmanship, such care paid to detail, such artistic beauty. To fully appreciate these items one wants to have these questions answered; a sense of their history is needed. Our pleasure and our skill in acquiring these items increases when we know more about them.

Since the dawn of history men have been making items out of clay to cook in and for use in storing their food and water. Clay is abundant and inexpensive, as old as time itself. It can be fashioned into a myriad of items taking almost any form man gives it and every culture in history has seemed to develop its own style and methods of pottery and its decoration. It has been said that porcelain is the highest expression of the potter's art and it is this same porcelain that continues to record a way of life for so many countries and cultures.

Nippon is not the name of the manufacturer as many think, but rather the country of origin. The word Nippon sounds like 'Neehon' in Japanese. It comes from a Chinese phrase meaning, "the source of the sun" and is the name the Japanese people called their country. This book deals with the pieces of Nippon porcelain manufactured in Japan for export during the years of 1891-1921.

Today, Nippon items are among the most sought after collectibles on the antique market. They're not antiques in the true sense of the word, not yet over 100 years old but most antique shops and shows have a supply for the collector.

As more and more people collect Nippon the cost of items seems to be skyrocketing. Just a few years ago a box full could be bought for just a few dollars. Not so anymore! Still, there are ways to obtain Nippon porcelain at reasonable prices if one has the time to shop. This includes visits to garage sales, thrift shops, flea markets and sometimes auctions or small out of the way antique shops. Very often a bargain can be found if the seller doesn't know the item's value. If you want some really nice items and get them at lower prices, my advice is just to get out and start looking for them. It's fine to pay today's high retail prices if you can afford them, but it's a lot more fun and easier on the pocketbook to make your own discoveries.

Sometimes, though, we just don't have the time or energy for this type of shopping so if circumstances permit and if you're willing to pay top dollar, build a repoire with a few reputable dealers. Let them know what you're looking for and they'll do the work for you. It's defintely a more expensive way to buy but I have found that it can be an excellent source to obtain some really choice pieces. Mail order can be another good source but ask for photos and a money-back guarantee. Buying through the mail can sometimes be difficult, even color pictures do not always show the item exactly and nothing is quite like seeing the real thing. Always ask for a warranty! The failure on any dealer's part to comply with this request would give me second thoughts.

Some pieces are definitely better than others as there are wide differences in quality. Some are more delicate, some have lavish gold overlay, some are embellished with beading, some are scenic, others floral, but all are old and most are quite beautiful. The majority of Nippon items are hand painted and say so on the mark.

Out of the thousands of pieces I have seen there have been only a few where even the pattern is the same. In fact, it has been a challenge trying to match pairs of vases and items that do have the same pattern.

Do not buy items that are chipped, cracked, have hairlines or repairs unless they are definitely lower in price. Check over each item before you make your purchase! The condition of the item should be of prime consideration. But, if you really love something and the price is reasonable, go ahead. I once bought a lovely cookie jar that had a chip on the rim. It was inexpensive and quite beautiful to look at. I bought it knowing full well that it would never command a very high price and probably not as much as I paid originally. Small hairlines or so-called spider marks are not as serious as chips and cracks but still should result in a lower price. One way to check if an item is cracked or been repaired is to use a long wave ultraviolet lamp. The majority of adhesives are clearly visible under black light and most repairs can be detected quite easily. These rays are harmless to the eyes and skin of the average healthy person and the lamps are available in portable models and most are moderately priced. In fact, one may prove to pay for itself many times over if defects are found in items before purchasing them.

It is ironic but today, most of us reject and find less desirable the Nippon items that are cracked or have been repaired. We want perfection! The Japanese have not always shared this same viewpoint, for in the earlier years in Japan, pieces of porcelain that had become broken were kept, mended and still cherished. The Japanese made no attempt to hide the cracks but instead accentuated them with gold lacquer. In fact, they felt this made the piece more interesting.

Question reliable dealers and collectors, gain from their knowledge and experience. Most will be very helpful if they have the information and most will tell you if they just do not know the answer. But, remember, listen with reservation. Just because someone says it's so, doesn't necessarily make it so. Even when all the 'so-called' experts agree, they too may be mistaken.

It is both frustrating and disappointing for one studying this porcelain to find that information is scant. I have written to so many sources in my quest for information simply to receive no answer. At times, investigation of the subject has seemed almost like a Herculean task. Records of the factories producing these wares were destroyed in World War II and the Morimura Bros. of New York City, an importer of these goods to our country, closed its doors in 1941.

My advice is to be informed and enlightened, read anything and everything you can on the subject. Go to the library, frequent museums, antique shops and shows, suscribe to weekly and monthly trade magazines and newspapers. Two museums in the United States having extensive Japanese ceramic collections are the Museum of Fine Arts in Boston and the Peabody Museum in Salem, Mass. The Peabody has an excellent collection of Japanese ceramics although only a small portion contains examples of export ware.

Collectors should continually upgrade their collections. Sell or trade off the minor pieces so that rarer items can be obtained. Our tastes change constantly and what appeals to us one year will not be as desirable the next. Each collector should also catalog his items. Pictures of each piece should be taken not only for future information but for protection against theft, fire, etc. A card file should be kept as well. List the item, price paid, date purchased and notate the condition, ex. worn, chipped, mint, etc.

In this book, I hope to acquaint the beginning collector with some of the different marks and items available and I'm sure the advanced collector will enjoy comparing his or her collection with the pieces shown. I have tried to select items which show the many different characteristics, designs, textures and shapes available in Nippon porcelain. Most pieces shown are those that the average collector can still obtain, however some rarer items have also been included. There seem to be as many different collections as collectors and each is typified by its exclusiveness.

Kyle Husfloen, Editor of the *Antique Trader* wrote an article on collecting that seems to sum up so many of my feelings. He was kind enough to give me permission to use it in this book.

Boredom and loneliness are probably two of the biggest mental health problems in modern day society. Senior citizens lose the will to go on living and youngsters go out and become delinquents simply because they are bored or lonely, or both. People in between these groups often spend empty evenings in front of the "boob tube" simply for lack of something creative to do. Many doctors have long prescribed developing outside interests or "hobbies" for patients whose physiological ailments may stem from psychological problems.

Who are some of the healthiest, happiest individuals around today? Probably members of the growing legion of collectors all over the country. Whether by accident or design, people who get interested in some facet of collecting are bound to find themselves getting involved with others of like interests and this will undoubtedly make for a better mental attitude.

Being able to share experiences and enthusiasm for your interests with those around you makes it easy to "come out" of yourself. A dedicated collector will undoubtedly find that as his or her interest in a field develops and grows, so will interest in other aspects of life. As you study and share your hobby with others you will probably find that life takes on new and added dimensions which were somehow missing before. As you search out your treasures at flea markets, shops or auctions you'll not only be getting physical exercise, but you'll be sharpening your senses and stimulating your thinking processes. even by just reading your favorite antiques publication or a good reference book you'll keep your brain active and alert.

Yes, there are probably very few serious collectors who are bored or lonely. They may become seriously afflicted with "antique-itis" or terminal "crippling of the billfold" but isn't that a better way to go than "cobwebs on the brain?" Promote mental health — start a collection today!

NIPPON

日本

The above characters stand for 'Nippon' (Japan), which is commonly referred to as 'Land of the Rising Sun'. According to the World Book Encyclopedia, the English version of this word is Nihon, however the i sounds like ee as in marine. The vowels are pronounced as they would be in Italian. The top character refers to the sun and the bottom means source. Together they make up the phrase 'the source of the sun' and so it is that the rays from this Japanese sun continue to light the corners of the world.

SEA OF OKHOTSK

HOKKAIDO

Hakodate

SOUTH KOREA

SEA OF JAPAN

Province of Kaga

HONSHU

Mt. Fuji

Tokyo (Yedo)

Korea Strait

Tsushima Strait

Kyoto

Nagoya

Yamato

Shimoda

Tokyo (Yedo) Bay

Arita Kiln

SHIKOKU

KYUSHU

PACIFIC OCEAN

EAST CHINA SEA

Province of Satsuma

Scale of Miles

0   50   100   150

Map of Japan showing approximate location of places mentioned in text.

6

History of Nippon

Nippon, "Land of the Rising Sun", a country of Oriental splendor. Legend tells us that the Japanese people descended from the Sun Goddess thousands of years ago, the sun being adored by the primitive Japanese. Japan, the oldest monarchy in the world, a chain of volcanic islands bordered by the Sea of Japan and the Pacific Ocean, off the coast of China. Its coast is deeply indented and the country consists of four main islands and thousands of smaller ones which span a length of about 1300 miles. It is a land of contrasts and contradictions. The bustle of Tokyo and the serenity of Kyoto. A land of tranquil palaces, temples and shrines. Waterfalls and lakes shimmer in the spectacular scenery of the snowcapped mountains. Ancient trees, lakes, valleys and rivers, the sun glittering over Mt. Fuji and yet it also can be a violent land at times, a land of earthquakes, hurricanes, typhoons, floods and volcanoes.

According to carbon dating, pottery making can be dated back to around 2500 B.C. in Japan. Jōmon was the name given to the people of this pottery culture, Jōmon meaning 'cord or rope pattern'. The clay pottery of these people was handshaped and marked with an overall rope pattern. The Jōmons were neolithic hunters and fishermen who disappeared around 250 B.C. Most of the Jōmon pottery that has been found was made with un-washed clay, often containing small pebbles. Cords were twisted, braided and knotted by the potter to obtain this design.

The so-called Yayoi people of the iron and bronze culture came into existence around 300-100 B.C. The Yayois were basically an agriculture people involved with acquatic rice cultivation. The Yayois were named after a suburb of Tokyo where the first discoveries of their wares were made. These people made most of their pottery in symmetrical shapes using the potter's wheel. The Yayoi wares were made with a more carefully washed clay than the Jōmons and their pottery has been found in more sizes and variety. They often used geometrical designs on their wares and they manufactured better goods than their predecessors. Both cultures' wares that have been found have been unglazed and been baked at low temperatures.

Tea was introduced in Japan from China in the 8th century. Tea at this time was a very costly item and when even small amounts were given to another it was treated as a precious gift. The tea was often stored in jars that were enclosed in bags of brocade. The Japanese tea ceremony, cha-no-yu, has always been both graceful and complex. Freshly ground tea was placed in a tea cup or small bowl of choice design. Hot water was added and the vessel was passed around from person to person, each carefully wiping it with a napkin after drinking the tea. Once the tea was finished the vessel was then passed around again so all could appreciate its beauty. This helped to stimulate the Oriental potters to produce lovelier works of art and had a definite effect on the making of Japanese pottery.

In 1638, Nippon was closed to all Europeans and cut off from the rest of the world. This was done to hopefully secure Japan from the Europeans and the rebellious Japanese peasants. The Japanese were forbidden to build any ship larger than a coasting boat. They could not go abroad and no foreigner could enter. The law of the land decreed a death penalty for any foreigner entering Japan and the people of Nippon lived in almost total seclusion for 214 years until Commodore Matthew Perry, USN, steamed into Yedo Bay in 1853. Yedo was later renamed Tokyo, meaning eastern capitol and this period of isolation in Japan is often referred to by historians as the Yedo period.

Perry arrived with four fighting ships, two steam frigates, the Mississippi (the flagship), and the Susquehanna, and two sloops named the Saratoga and the Plymouth. He was sent to deliver President Fillmore's letter which was written in the hope of establishing trade and friendship between the United States and Japan. The United States needed harbors in which to dock its ships for repairs and supplies and wanted better treatment for shipwrecked sailors. Upon arrival in Nippon, Perry sent messages to the Japanese dignitaries but received only short and un-satisfactory answers in return. They attempted to send minor officials to deal with him but he refused. At one point he even threatened to land with armed forces if an answer was not soon forthcoming. Reluctantly, he withdrew his boats and troops for the winter with the promise of returning in the spring for his answer. This time, upon his arrival in February of 1854, he was met in a much friendlier fashion. This was more than likely due to the fact that he now appeared with ten ships instead of four. They were all powered by steam amd mounted with many large guns. The Japanese referred to them as the 'Black Ships', because of the clouds of black smoke they produced. These clouds could be seen all over the countryside and the Japanese were undoubtedly impressed with this display of force. Perry proceeded to play upon their fears. This time they put up no resistance and before long trade negotiations were underway. The Kanagawa treaty, opening the small ports of Shimoda near the Bay of Yedo and Hakodate in the north was signed on March 31, 1854. Shipwrecked sailors were to receive good treatment and an American Consul was permitted to reside at Shimoda. Soon, treaties with other European countries followed. By

1865, Japan was opened to world trade and ensuing contacts with the West brought a flood of European art to her shores. Japan had thus been 'rediscovered', her seclusion was ended and a new life began.

The Japanese have always had an eagerness to learn from others and now native painters went abroad to study and learn the ways of the new world. It has been said that the Japanese are 'conscious cultural borrowers', they seem to have the capacity to borrow and adapt, making it something new and quintessentially Japanese. They merely reshaped everything to suit their needs.

During this period the Japanese government also hired thousands of foreign experts to come to Japan to train their people. The artists began imitating the European styles or tried to combine both those of the Eastern and Western manner. There were no copyright laws and the Japanese copied whatever they admired. They were highly skilled and capable of quickly learning new techniques. They had previously copied the master artists from China but in order to satisfy this new Western market they now copied the arts of many other countries. Occidental decoration was being painted on Oriental wares.

The Japanese had a famous capacity for imitation and today we find Nippon porcelain that resembles Limoges, Beleek, Wedgwood, Gouda, Royal Bayreuth, RS Prussia, the list goes on and on. All types of items were manufactured from elaborately decorated vases and punch bowl sets to plain utilitarian items such as butter tubs and juicers. One finds dolls, incense burners and souvenir items, so varied was the market. Thus, the country of Nippon began world trade and porcelain became one of her major export items.

The Japanese first exhibited in the West at the International Exhibition in London in 1862. They also exhibited at the Centennial Exhibition of 1876 in Philadelphia, the Paris Exhibition in 1878 and the Columbian Exposition in Chicago in 1893 had a large exhibit of Japanese items. The new styles and patterns took the West by storm and for a number of years everyone went Japanese mad. The country of Nippon now began to enjoy unprecedented prosperity.

In 1868, Emperor Mutsuhito, mounted the throne beginning the Meiji period, meaning enlightened rule, which was to continue until his death in 1912. (Each ruler took a name for his reign and Japanese emperors were known by their reign name.) The feudal system was suppressed in 1871 marking the rise of the upper middle classes led by the powerful trading families. Previously, the merchant had been placed at the bottom of the social scale but now began to dominate economic life.

During this time Japan continued to be seized with a mania for anything 'Western'. What we did not know was that it was not an underdeveloped country as we had thought but one that was highly advanced. Its development had merely followed non-Western lines. Japan now sought to catch up and bring the level of her culture to that of the Western countries and by 1899 she found herself equal to the most advanced European powers. Factories had been erected, steamships built, a universal school system was established and feudalism abolished. Pottery factories were promoted and the first railway line in Japan was opened in 1872 helping to give rise to the increased trade. Within one lifetime the Meiji government increased trade, developed industries and created an army and navy to match that of Russia's. Japan had adapted to Westernism in order to meet the West on more even terms and gain its respect.

At this time, however, Japan also found herself with a minimum of land and an over abundance of labor. There were approximately 40 million prople living in Japan in 1891, by 1909 this figure had risen to 50 million. Industry kept growing and the search for overseas markets for goods became vital. Low wages were paid to almost all of the workers, the employers claimed this was necessary to enable them to compete more effectively. Japan's prices were thus kept low enabling her to sell goods all over the world.

Pottery techniques and styles had developed down through the centuries in Japan. Generation after generation of people had practiced these skills and passed them onto their children. The Japanese, however, generally looked upon export porcelain as inferior to that made for Japanese use, as their tastes and likes were more for pottery items and the very simple designs. They attached little emphasis to ornamentation in their early period and decorated their wares sparingly. In fact, Oriental cups were handleless and the Japanese preferred a flat contour plate to one with a rim. The broad rims were for Western export only. In Japan, tablewares not intended for export were sold in sets of five and many times even each cup in a set was decorated differently form the others. Pairs of vases were contrary to Japanese taste. Gaudy decoration was more important to the West and in an attempt to please the foreign buyer, Japan gave the West what it wanted to buy. The rising demand from Europe and America led to styles alien to the native tastes of Japan.

Modern factory equipment was installed, plaster molds were introduced and European methods of glazing were tried. Previously the kilns had been fired by wood, now coal and oil were used. Whole villages made pottery and decorated it, in fact, children were used to decorate many of the Nippon wares. By the time the 1900's rolled around assembly line techniques were already being employed in the making of Nippon porcelain.

Most of the artists are anoymous to us as few signed their name to their works of art. The hands that fashioned these items often times expended much skill, taste and time in their behalf and one can almost envision the artist holding a piece of porcelain and decorating it in a way he felt would be pleasing.

In October of 1890, the McKinley Tariff Act was passed by Congress, named for Rep. William McKinley who sponsored it. McKinley drafted this bill at the insistence of the Easterners in the United States who wanted more protection for US manufacturers. The tariff act of the Fifty-First Congress stated the following:

> Chapter 1244, Section 6: "That on and after the first day of March, eighteen hundred and ninety-one, all articles of foreign manufacture, such as are usually or ordinarily marked, stamped, branded or labeled, and all packages containing such or other imported articles, shall, respectively, be plainly marked, stamped, branded or labeled in legible English words, so as to indicate the country of their origin; and unless so marked, stamped, branded or labeled they shall not be admitted to entry".

In March of 1921, the government reversed its position and decided that the word Nippon was a Japanese word, the English equivalent of which is Japan. Customs agents were then instructed that as of Sept. 1, 1921, merchandise from Japan, the marking of which is governed by this provision of law, should not be released when bearing only the Japanese word "Nippon" to indicate the country of origin. Thus the era of Nippon covered in this book was over.

The Japanese items were less expensive to purchase than pieces coming from Germany or Austria and around the end of the nineteenth and early into the twentieth century were very popular in the United States. This country was very receptive to the inexpensive porcelain and as a result much was imported. Many of the items were sold in gift shops, at summer resorts, boardwalks, fairs, five and ten cent stores, carnivals, penny arcades and even at the local grocery store.

Montgomery Ward was founded in 1872 and by 1890 offered 2,400 items for sale in its catalog. Woolworths opened in 1879 and Sears and Roebuck originated in 1893. Rural Free Delivery, 1896, and Parcel Post, 1913, enabled manufacturers to sell directly to the farmers without middlemen. Mass retailing such as the mail order houses, the chains and the department stores, which often purchased directly from the manufacturer, also contributed to this simpler and more efficient distribution.

It is interesting to note how much Nippon porcelain items actually sold for during this period. The 1908 Sears catalog lists vases for $.59 each, a nine piece tea set sold for $2.29, game plates were $.95 a dozen and cups and saucers were sold as low as $1.49 a dozen.

Of course, other prices were also low along with the wages of this time period. Bedroom suites sold for $14.95, ladies dresses were $1.48 and one could buy house paint for $.39 a gallon. This paint came with a ten year guarantee and a large two story home could be painted for about $4.00. Wouldn't we all love to find such bargains today!

During the years of 1870-1900 the American export trade nearly tripled. There was an increasing demand for a greater world market. This era in US history knew strikes, depressions, as well as buoyancy and free spending. Items which had previously been available only to the wealthy were now available to the middle class. During this so called 'Gilded Age' there was incredible business expansion. It was a time of skyscrapers, steam engines, railroads, telephones and telegraphs. The period of 1891 to 1921 was certainly an historic making time in our country's history. The United States faced financial panic, the San Francisco earthquake and fire, the Wright Bros. first flight, the sinking of the Titantic, the first ship passing through the Panama Canal, Women's suffrage and World War I.

In the late 1800's, Britain was the most powerful country in the world and was under the rule of Queen Victoria. Queen Victoria reigned longer than any other English monarch and from 1837 to 1901 she exerted political and social pressure throughout the world. The late Victorian Age was a time for ostentation, ornate, fancy, even exotic items, a time when knick-knacks abounded. It was a time of past elegance. Japanese art reached peaks of popularity in Europe and during the late Victorian Age the pieces became gaudier and gaudier until almost every square inch was covered with decoration. The people of this era identified decoration with beauty, the more ornate and intricate the design the better. On many of the Nippon wares, the design tends to cover the article which appealed to the English at this particular time in history and as a result much of this inexpensive porcelain ware was imported from Japan.

The decade from 1912-1926 greeted a new emperor in Japan, Yoshihito, who took the name of Taisho, meaning great peace. This was a period much like the one that had preceded it. Increased trade continued with Japan and she found herself adapting easily to the foreign cultural influences.

Table Manners & Customs
At the turn of the century

Grandmother lived quite differently than we do today. Even the assortment of dishes she used back in the Victorian era varies considerably from the items we now use. Because of this, we often find a Nippon porcelain article only to wonder what it possibly could have been used for. Others are familiar to us but rarely used today.

Some of the harder to find Nippon items include cuspidors (spitoons), kniferests, hanging hatpin holders, individual condiment sets, egg warmers, and mustache cups to mention a few. How little knowledge most of us have of old table manners and furnishings and we can learn so much about a past people from studying the dishes they used.

Cuspidors were household necessities back in the days when snuff for the ladies and chewing tobacco for the men was so popular. Snuff is a dried powdered tobacco which was inserted into the nostrils. This made expectoration a necessity and the little spitoons were used by the ladies. Some were very elaborately hand painted and were small enought to be held in the hand. Some had handles and the very smallest spitoon is referrred to as a spittle cup.

Knife rests were popular during the Victorian era and many can be found in the shape of miniature dumbbells while others look like a miniature saw horse with scrolly legs. Large ones held the blade of the carving knife and fork near the platter and smaller ones were placed at each diner's plate. They were originally used to prevent the tablecloth from being soiled.

Mustaches and beards were in vogue in the late 1800's and the need for a mustache cup becomes readily apparent. After the Civil War the handlebar mustache became the rage in this country. The cup came in all sizes from demitasse to extra large and had a bar across the top to keep the mustache out of the coffee or beverage. The mustache rested on this lid and was kept dry. A left handed mustache cup is a rarity.

It was also stylish at this time to use napkin rings when dining. The well appointed tables of this era had one at the table for each member of the family. Nippon ones can be found in an assortment of patterns and it can be quite a challenge trying to collect a complete matching set.

The sugar shaker or so-called muffineer was popular from the late 1800's until World War I. It held sugar or cinnamon for use at the dinner table. Sugar was sifted on certain foods such as doughnuts, berries or grapefruit much as we use salt shakers of today. The sugar shaker is generally high domed and holds about a cup of sugar.

Potpourri jars, the word being derived from the French. A porpourri jar was used to scent a room and contained a mixture of spiced flower petals. It was a practice introduced in the late 18th century and continued well into the late Victorian period. There were also cricket jars which of course, held crickets. The top had small slits in it to give the crickets air and allowed one to listen to their sounds.

Match holders and matchbox holders were popular from 1860 to the early 1900's. Matches were scarce and expensive back then and the holders kept the matches dry and safe. Some match holders even had scratchers on them. Many were hung on the wall, some sat on a table or desk and some were part of a smoke set.

Smoking sets generally contained a tray along with three or four other items, a covered humidor, an ashtray, matchbox or matchstick holder and cigarette holder. The humidors used with these sets tend to be of a smaller size, under 6" in height and in scale with the size of the set. I have seen the trays in 3 shapes round, oval and diamond. Smoking sets were popular from 1900 to 1920 amd most are found decorated in very masculine motifs, ships, cigars and pipes, scenes, etc. Of course, whenever you have an item that is composed of several pieces the chances that all the pieces will be found intact is slim. Smoking sets, desk sets and dresser sets were put out to be used every day and very often a piece or two became broken. Tea sets and chocolate sets were generally stored in china cabinets, used less often and usually cared for better.

Dresser sets usually consisted of a tray, hatpin holder, hair receiver, toothbrush holder, powder box and sometimes a talcum powder container and perhaps a ring tree and stickpin holder. Other boudoir accessories included a rose bowl, jewel box or trinket box, cologne bottles, fern dishes and often candlesticks.

The stickpin holder is small, generally from 1½" to 2¼" high. Years ago men wore stickpins instead of the tie clips and tie tacks of today. The stickpin holder generally has fewer holes on top than hatpin holders and looks like a small version of a salt shaker. Some can be found with attached underplates. This item is rare and tends to be quite high in price. Ladies hatpin holders are sometimes mistaken for the sugar shaker which is generally fatter in shape and has a high domed top. Nippon hanging hatpin holders are rare to find. Ring holders or ring trees were used in the bedroom, bath, even the kitchen, wherever one removed their rings. The saucer underneath was used for cufflinks, blouse pins, etc. Many were manufactured in the shape of a hand outstretched from the saucer. The hand is in an upright position with the fingers spread apart. Others can be found in the shape of a 'tree' with outstretched branches, still others are combination pieces of ring trees and hatpin holders. Hair receivers consist of two pieces. The receiver has a hole in the center of the top piece which was used to hold the strands of hair from the brush or comb after grooming one's hair.

Inkwells were often part of a desk set. They were found in schools, offices and homes and made of all kinds of materials and into all kinds of shapes. Nippon ones range from the very ornate to the very plain. The development of the ball point pen in 1930 made inkwells almost obsolete. Desk sets usually consisted of an inkwell, ink blotter, letter holder, stamp box and tray. Some however, even came with calendar holders and porcelain blotter corners.

Another item not often found today is the butter pat or butter chip. Years ago each person had his own individual butter pat at the dinner table on which his butter was placed. It was also very fashionable at restaurants and hotels from the late 19th century but gradually waned out in the 40's. The butter pat has now been replaced with the bread and butter plate. Sometimes the butter pat is confused with coasters or individual salts (which are usually smaller and deeper) or children's doll dishes. A butter pat is generally not more than 3½" wide and basically is flat with a slope on the edges.

Punchbowls just naturally mean hospitality and good cheer. Many were gaily flowered and ornately decorated. We owe the punch or pauch bowl to the Orientals. Pauch was a drink originating in India. It consists of five ingredients, lemon juice, arrack, tea, sugar and water. Many Nippon punch bowls are two piece items and come with matching cups. A favorite pattern seems to be the one using grapes and grape leaves as decoration.

The teapot conveys a cozy feeling and afternoon tea was a custom in many homes. Coffee was generally served after dinner when everyone retired to the drawing room. Both coffee and tea services consisted of the pot, creamer, sugar bowl, cups and saucers and often a serving tray. A small plate for lemon slices was used when serving tea.

Bone dishes were also part of a dinner set in the late Victorian period. They were crescent shaped dishes placed in front of each diner for fish or chicken bones.

Condensed milk containers are another choice item. They usually had an underplate and always had a hole in the bottom to aid in removing the container. Slant top cheese dishes, watermelon sets, corn sets, asparagus and ice cream sets were also made. There was Nippon porcelain to fit every need.

Game sets and fish sets very often consisted of 12 plates with a serving platter. The game sets can be found decorated with animals, wild birds and turkeys. The fish sets were often decorated with fish, lobsters or shells.

Children's feeding dishes are another unusual item to be found. Some were sectioned and all were decorated to appeal to the small child, some with fairy tale and nursery rhyme or cartoon characters. Children's play dishes were also decorated with these same whimsical patterns. There were even children's dresser sets containing a hatpin holder about two inches in height, a hair receiver which was just a little smaller and a ring tree which was only about an inch and a quarter tall. Today these children's items are quite rare and many are expensive when found. Little girls had copies of whatever mother had. There were also the tiny doll's dishes meant for dolly when she had her tea party and rarest of all the miniature doll house dishes. All these were provided for the little girl not only for her pleasure but also to learn the social graces of entertaining.

Centuries ago, salt was coveted by royalty and was traded equal amounts for gold. It was also used as a means of exchange. The first patent for a salt shaker as we know it was issued in 1863. It was invented so that we might sprinkle the salt on our food rather than using individual salt dishes. Most Nippon salt shakers have a cork in the bottom but some can be found with a screw top. In 1858, John Mason invented the jar with screw threads molded in the glass (Mason jars) and led the way for screw top salt shakers.

Back in the Victorian era when one was received at the door of the host, you handed your calling card to the maid or attendant. She in turn took the card to the person being visited. At receptions and large parties one left his calling card and invitation on a card tray in the hall. Most Nippon calling card trays found today are quite ornamental and gaudy in decoration. It seems that there is so much to be learned of our ancestor's past manners and customs.

Teacup & Saucer

Chocolate Cup
& Saucer

After-Dinner
Coffee Cup & Saucer

Both May Have Cover

2 Handled
Bouillon Cup
& Saucer

Handleless
Bouillon Cup
& Saucer

Tea Strainer
With Bottom

Teapot, Shorter In Height
Have Long Spouts, Always Has Cover

Black Coffee Pot
Tall With Long Spout
Always Has Cover

Chocolate Pot
Tall With Short Spout
Always Has Cover

Milk Pitchers, Generally Medium In
Height, Short Spout, Some Have Covers

Profiles of some of the different shapes of pots and cups found. Many a novice collector doesn't know the difference between a chocolate and a coffee pot, how to tell a demitasse cup from a chocolate cup, etc. A chocolate pot is distinguished from a coffee pot by its short spout, a bouillon cup is either two handled or handleless, some bouillon cups even have covers. The after dinner coffee cup or demitasse is the smallest of all, the chocolate cup is tall and narrow. Many of the cups have a pedestal shaped base.

The Manufacture of Nippon Porcelain

The word porcelain is said to have been derived from the Italian word 'porcellana', meaning cowry shell. The Chinese ware which was brought back to Venice in the 15th century was thought to resemble the pearly coating of this shell and thus the name porcellana was given to it. The French adaption of the word is porcelaine.

Hard paste is a true porcelain originating a long time ago in China around the year 800 A.D. It was a mixture of kaolin and chinastone which was fired at a very high temperature. For centuries the Chinese concealed the secret of making porcelain. The word kaolin originates from the Chinese word Kao-ling meaning 'the high hills', which were near the ancient city of Ching-tê-Chên. Here, nearly a million Chinese people lived and almost all were devoted to the making of porcelain. This China ware was then sent approximately four hundred miles away to Canton for export. The term porcelain is often used interchangeably by collectors with 'China ware', this name of course, being derived from the country of origin where it was originally manufactured.

The Chinese often stored their finished wares for decades before using them, as porcelain strength and hardness tends to increase with age. In fact, they also buried their clay to season it. They felt that the older clay became the better it was to work with.

Porcelain is composed mainly of kaolin and petuntse. Kaolin is a highly refractory natural white clay which makes the mixture more pliable and plastic. However, it is not fusible even at the highest temperatures. Petuntse is a clay found in felspathic rocks such as granite. This ingredient makes the mixture more fusible and durable. When fired together they strengthen each other and fuse into porcelain. Porcelain can be eggshell thin or thick enough for furniture. Although it may appear quite delicate and thin, it is actually quite strong and durable, it is also resistant to heat, acids and staining. It is translucent and when held up to a light one can see rays of light through the article. Porcelain, however, never becomes transparent no matter how high a temperature it is fired at. Many of the Nippon pieces have a pure white background while others tend to have a very light gray colored appearance. Actually, the gray color tended to blend easier with most designs.

Porcelain has a fine deep ring (a clear bell-like note) when tapped with the finger; cracked pieces do not ring so this is a test we can give items before purchasing them. The more kaolin used in the porcelain the harder it becomes and most porcelain made since the late 19th century contains more kaolin than the earlier wares. The hardness of porcelain can be tested in the following way — take a piece of broken porcelain, put a drop of ink or dye on the rough edge and the ink can still be easily removed. On earthenware, the ink is readily absorbed.

In the early 1700's, Johanne F. Böttger, a young alchemist working in Germany discovered the value of using kaolin to produce porcelain. In Europe, kaolin was originally used for wig powder and cosmetics. Böttger supposedly came across some of the white hair powder, suspected it might be a clay and experimented with it. How much of this story is actually true I'm not quite sure, but Böttger is credited with the discovery of kaolin in Europe and this helped to revolutionize the china making industry there. He became a famous potter making molds of the Chinese wares and using his clay to make replicas.

Pottery in its broadest sense includes porcelain as well as other forms of ceramic wares, the difference being the raw ingredients used and the methods of firing. With all forms, however, clay is the most important raw material to the potter and Japan's mountains provide her with an almost unlimited supply of clay. The mountains are made of granite rock and over the course of time the granite got washed down the mountain and was left deposited at the bottom. The Japanese were very fortunate as few places in Japan are very far from the mountains or very distant from the sea. The mountains providing the clay and the water allowing for easy exportation of the finished wares.

History can trace the use of the potter's wheel back to the Egyptians over four thousand years ago and since the Yayoi culture many of the earlier Japanese pieces were made on such a wheel. The basic idea behind the potter's wheel is to make better items in a shorter period of time. The potter merely throws a ball of clay onto the center of the rotating wheel, keeping the clay moisturized at all times. The clay must be in a plastic state and the force of the wheel and the thrust of the potter's hands are capable of producing many types of cylindrical objects.

Among the types of molds that are used for making pottery items are press molds, sprig molds, drape or flopover molds, solid casting molds and drain molds.

A sprig mold is a one piece mold which is used in making sprigging ornaments or any type of item where only one side of the piece is molded. The decoration is incised into the mold. Moist clay is rolled out and squeezed into the mold until every bit of the plaster mold is filled. The excess clay is scraped off with a modeling tool. After the item has dried it is carefully lifted out. The finished item will be the exact reverse of the mold, whatever is incised into the mold will protrude out on the porcelain piece. Only the one side is molded and the exposed side becomes the back of the finished item. Liquid or casting slip may also be poured into sprig molds in place of the plastic clay.

When used as a sprigging ornament, both figures and vessels must be dampened with water or liquid clay to make them adhere. Only slight pressure is needed as too much might spoil the detail of the ornament.

Press molds are often used to make figurines and handles. Primitive press molds were often shells and gourds and press molds were used in China as early as 206 B.C. A press mold is much like a sprig mold only it requires two pieces rather than one. Soft clay is put into each half of the mold. The two pieces are pressed together, the excess clay if scraped off and the item is removed from the mold upon drying. Items that have been cast from a mold with two or more pieces have slight ridge marks (also called fettles) where the sections of the mold are joined at the seam. They are merely scraped or filed off and generally wiped with a wet sponge.

Drain molds are used in making vases, cups, hollow ware, jars, etc. Liquid slip is poured in the mold until the desired thickness of the walls is acheived. The excess clay is then poured out. The porous plaster absorbs some of the water and leaves a 'wall' of partially dried clay. The hollow piece is allowed to remain in the mold until it becomes hard enough to be removed. The clay will start to shrink and separate from the mold when it is ready. Some items can be made in a one piece drain mold provided the shape is widest at the top of the item. When using a one piece mold the item always has to be absolutely level across the top.

Widest Part   This   Not This   Widest Part

Two piece molds are used when the widest part of the design is somewhere between the top and the bottom of the item. More intricate designs are acheived by using more mold pieces. The parts of the mold are removed when the clay is leather hard (also called cheese hard). Again, slight ridges are formed where the pieces of the mold meet and must be scraped off or fettled. A drain mold is always made in the shape of the outside of the item to be molded.

Solid casting molds are used for items such as shallow bowls and plates. In this type of mold, the thickness of the walls is determined by the mold and every piece is formed identically, a definite advantage over the drain mold. Solid casting can be done with either liquid slip or plastic clay. The mold shapes both the inside and the outside of the piece and the thickness of the walls is controlled. Plates and bowls generally require a two piece mold but some wares have to be built up of a number of separately molded pieces. The range is practically endless in what can be produced. When using a mold, all pieces must fit exactly, they are fitted together and then tied. Items made in molds of more than one piece are removed by simply taking apart the mold piece by piece.

A drape or flopover mold is used only when making flat bottomed items such as ashtrays, plates and platters. Moist clay is rolled out and draped over the mold and pressed firmly into shape. The item is trimmed with a modeling tool and when it dries is tapped loose from the mold.

Some pieces after being taken from the molds are still in a somewhat plastic state and are then further shaped by hand. You can often feel a piece and see how the potter has shaped the ware between his thumb and fingers. Porcelain greenware warps easily and great care had to be exerted when working with it.

The Japanese soon discovered that plaster molds were the best to use as the plaster of paris absorbs the water from the clay and helps it to dry out quickly.

The jigger and jolley were also utilized in making porcelain wares. A jigger is a machine resembling a potter's wheel. Soft clay is placed onto a convex shaped mold, the mold being located on a turntable or wheel. As the wheel turns, a template is held against it trimming off the excess clay on the outside to form a predetermined shape. The revolving mold shapes the inside of the item such as a plate and the template cuts the outside. The clay must be pressed firmly with the template and the wheel must be kept in motion at all times.

A jolley is much like a jigger only in reverse. It is used more commonly for bowls and cups. The mold for the bowls is concave and the template forms the inside of the item. The template is lowered inside the revolving mold, the mold forming the outside surface while the template cuts the inside. However, neither the jigger or jolley can easily produce items that are irregularly shaped.

After the items have been carefully dried they are fired. The greenware (unfired clay) shrinks twice, once in drying and again in the firing. As the temperature in the kiln rises, the water in the clay is vaporized. Each type of clay has a different maturing temperature when fired and porcelain is capable of being fired to temperatures of 2360°-2750°F or approximately 1300°-1500°C. Exposing clay to this extreme heat causes it to change from a soft pliable material to one that is hard and brittle.

Porcelain items require a high temperature glaze and the body and glaze join together as one during the firing process. This glaze cannot be chipped or flaked off. Porcelain left unglazed is called biscuit or bisque. Items that are glazed are impervious to liquids, unglazed items are more porous.

There are several types of decoration found on Nippon wares, among them are underglaze colors which were applied before glazing and firing. Colored glazes were also used to cover a piece with a single color. So many Nippon items were formed identically by the potter that the decoration was the one thing that made each item unique.

Glazes can be traced back to Egypt, 3500-3000 B.C. and are composed of silica, alumina and flux. Each glaze has different characteristics and various temperatures at which it must be fired. If the glaze and body expand at different rates, the glaze will either crack or fall off. Many times the clay and glaze require different temperatures so different firings must be done for each. Glazes can be painted on, sprayed, poured on or dipped on. They vary in texture and can range from a matte to bright glossy to the sheen of luster. Luster glazes have a metallic pigment, silver, gold, etc. Real metal was used including copper and platinum and this metallic luster had to be fired at lower temperatures than most other glazes. The luster glazes tend to be used later in the Nippon period and most of the Japanese luster work found today was made after 1921. When gold was used on white it produced a lilac or metallic pink, silver luster was made from platinum and copper produces a gold or copper brown look.

The matte or dull glaze has a low reflectance (doesn't get sharp highlights) when fired and it must have a slow cooling cycle or it may become to shiny.

During the firing process the glazed pieces must never touch each other or any part of the kiln. The glaze bubbles up and if the pieces are too close they will ultimately stick to each other. The glaze melts into a liquid and upon cooling is hardened into a vitreous coating.

Stilts are used in the kiln to separate and support the items but tend to leave impressions on the underside of the glazed ware. These marks must eventually be ground smooth. Many items were left unglazed on the bottom because they had no feet on which to stand.

In examining pieces from the Nippon era we notice that some have holes drilled in them. These holes allowed the steam to escape when the item was being fired in the kiln. Other items will have a bar or raised design molded on the bottom of the piece of the porcelain. These gave the piece additional support and helped to prevent stress cracks.

Early Nippon items had their handles and finials made separately and these were later attached to the body of the article. When pieces were attached, the handles, spouts, etc. had to be at the same degree of hardness or else they might fall off or crack. All pieces had to dry out at the same rate.

In the later Nippon period when Nippon ware was being mass produced there were people who had jobs just attaching handles and knobs. The knobs, feet and legs were originally put on for convenience, however, as the years passed they also became quite ornamental. Many times though balls of clay were merely attached to the bottom of items to produce feet.

Often times everything was included in the same mold, making it a more economical process. If the handle was made separately and later attached, the body of the item will be smooth inside. When both are made together in one mold, the handles appear to be drawn up out of the body, sometimes there is a hole showing on the inside of the item which makes the handle or finial appear to be hollow or semi-hollow.

In the earlier Nippon pieces before the age of mass production we find that a matched pair of vases are not really identical. One may be a little taller and the painting may vary a little on each. These so-called imperfections do not detract from the item but only serve to enhance its beauty and add to its desirability to the collector.

With many of the hand painted items, the artist was merely given a model to follow and was expected to reproduce the design. Many of the commercially produced wares were hand painted by workers following outlines printed on the plain china, the design being stenciled on first before painting. During the later Nippon period, a number of individuals probably worked on each piece much like our assembly lines of today. Still, this type of decoration was slow and the demand for services of the artists often exceeded the supply. The art work, of course, varied from piece to piece depending on the skill of the artist. Mass production increased during this time and the earlier pieces tend to be more individualistic and generally of a higher quality. They display more hand painting and finer brushwork than the latter ones.

DaVinci once wrote "If the painter wishes to see enchanting beauties, he has the power to produce them. If he wishes to see monstrosities, whether terrifying, or ludicrous and laughable, or pitiful, he has the power and authority to create them. If he wishes to produce towns or deserts, if in the hot season he wants cool and shady places, or in the cold season warm places, he can make them. If he wants valleys, if from high mountaintops he wants to survey vast stretches of country, if beyond he wants to see the horizon on the sea, he has the power to create all this; and likewise from deep valleys and beaches. Indeed, whatever exists in the universe, whether in essence, in act, or in the imagination, the painter has first in his mind and then in his hands. His hands are of such excellence that they can present to our view simultaneously well-proportioned harmonies real things exhibit piecemeal!". Such is our legacy in these Nippon hand painted wares.

15

Helpful Hints On How To Care For Your Nippon Porcelain

Everyone has their own ideas on how something should be cared for and I find that I am no exception. Most of what I have learned has come to me through advice from other collectors or dealers, by reading how-to books and my own 'tragic' accidents.

First rule, don't leave items out where they can get knocked over or accidently hit. Keep them out of the reach of small children and family pets. Stop accidents before they happen!

I would suggest washing your items carefully, do not put a lot of pieces in the sink at one time. I use warm softened water for both the washing and rinsing of my articles. Don't use abrasives or scouring pads as this will often wear off some of the decoration. If an item is real dirty a good long soaking in water and soap will usually correct the problem. If not take a stiff bottle brush to scrub it clean.

Don't use chlorine bleach on your hand painted items! I know some people prefer this method but it stands to reason that the item will have to lose some of its vibrant colors when soaked. If the white gets whiter the colors must get duller. Discolored hairlines can sometimes be cleaned with a dab of chlorine on a cotton swab. If the line is not too dirty some of the discoloration may disappear but this is only a temporary measure.

Some authorities also believe that cracks can be boiled clean, however, I try to never subject my items to great changes in temperature.

For the Pickard gold etched items the factory suggests "Only simple care is needed to keep Pickard Gold China in beautiful condition. To remove stains simply wash the piece thoroughly using a mild soap in warm water or an ammonia type glass cleaner. Do not use silver polish, steel wool or harsh cleaning powders."

Most of us seem to have a multitude of dishes, far more than we can ever need or use. Hence, these items have to be stored and we should be careful to store them properly.

Dishes should always be separated with napkins, paper, felt or doilies, etc. Items that are unglazed on the bottom may not only scratch each other but our furniture as well so it would be advisable to be careful when placing these pieces on your wooden or glass furniture.

Cups shouldn't be stacked on top of one another as there is always the risk of chipping. Also don't hang them by their handles as this is their weakest point.

When we store things in boxes we must be extra careful. I have found that disposable diapers or hospital pads make great wrappers and provide adequate protection. Whenever mailing items, a good suggestion would be to use these wrappers and double box. Both boxes should be filled with styrofoam or sufficient newspaper to cut down on damage.

Buy the best you can afford initially. Check to see that the item is in good condition, free of cracks, hairlines, repairs, etc. This type of item will only increase in value for you.

But, of course there is always the occasion when we break one of our favorite items or succumb and purchase a piece that is not perfect. If the item is valuable take it to a professional restorer. Ask him what he can do with it. Will it look as before and is the cost of the repair justified? If not and you still want to keep the item, try putting it back together yourself. A good how-to book would be a good start. Study the pieces to see how they fit together. Perhaps you could first practice on an item which is of little value.

Porcelain dishes are actually quite a bit stronger and more durable than most people know but accidents can happen. Use them and enjoy them but treat them with tender loving care. They represent a past life and it is our responsibility to try to pass them down to future generations. They are not only lovely to look at but most important of all they are irreplaceable.

Designs And Techniques Used On Nippon Items

There are a variety of shapes, designs and decorations to be found on Nippon porcelain. Some pieces have overall designs and many vases have landscapes that literally go all the way around the vase; there is no beginning and no end although there is generally less detail on the reverse side. Middle East scenes with pyramids, palm trees, camels and deserts were popular during the early period in which Nippon was manufactured. The style seems to lie somewhere between a mixture of both East and West. River scenes, Greek key patterns, geometric designs, weeping willow trees, flowering shrubs and buds are but a few we find.

Gold was used quite lavishly on the pieces exported during the Meiji period (1868-1912). However, much of this gold was not very durable and today we find that a number of these pieces have much of the gold worn off. Some dealers and collectors have a tendency to add gold paint to these items but generally it can be detected quite easily. I personally feel that this detracts from the item and it is best to leave it alone. When one sees an item that is worn at least we know that it had been used often and probably been cared about a great deal.

Some pieces of Nippon are decorated in a Moriage design. Sandra Andacht wrote the folowing information in the December 28, 1977 issue of *The Antique Trader Weekly*, Dubuque, Iowa. She allowed me to reprint much of her article. "An English interpretation of the word 'Moriage' (pronunciation: MORE-EE-A-GAY) is "to pile up." When this definition is applied to Japanese ceramics, it refers to applied clay (slip) relief decorations. These decorations are found on many classes of Japanese pottery and porcelain articles. This type of ornamentation has been used for over two hundred years and is quite predominant on export wares, produced since the Nippon era (1891-1921), and through to World War II.

There are three basic methods for applying Moriage designs. One method is hand rolling and shaping. With this method, the clay is applied by hand, to the biscuit, in one or more layers. The thickness and shaping of the clay is dependent upon the design and the visual effect required.

The second and more conventional method, made use of tubing. Before the advent of rubber, bamboo tubing was used. The tubing was filled with softened clay (slip) and was trailed onto the biscuit in much the same manner as one would decorate a cake. This method may also be called 'slip trailing'. Quite often the slip trailed design has a series of raised ridges (e.g: slip trailed dragon).

With the third technique, the slip is reduced to a liquified state, so that it may be manipulated with a brush. This technique is referred to as 'Hakemé', by the Japanese.

Moriage designs may be applied either before or after glazing. The clay (slip) may be treated with color either before or after application. Often the designs are slightly enameled over, especially when outlining is needed, or a lacy effect is desired. Most often the moriage designs are matted and the backgrounds of the wares on which they appear have variegated tones and muted hues. This lends more depth to the applied designs and is quite effective visually.

Moriage designs are innumerable and varied. They include border trimmings, lacy designs, floral motifs, birds, animals and landscapes.

The companies that used Moriage decorations are numerous. Some of the marks found on Moriage adorned wares are: Green M in Wreath Nippon, Blue Maple Leaf Nippon, and Royal Moriye Nippon. It is important to remember that Moriye (Royal Moriye Nippon) was merely the name of a company, which used Moriage designs on many of its wares. However, it would be "improper" to use the name of a company in lieu of the decoration.

The Moriage design with the highest availability and the most popularity is the jewel-eyed, slip trailed dragon. The dragon motif has been used extensively since the middle of the Nippon era. Many base values on accessibility. However, this should not be the sole factor for determining value. Consideration must be given to the intensity and intricacy of the design and the overall detailing. As with other Oriental art forms, one piece may have been decorated by one or more artists and, in most instances, with great care. Therefore workmanship is a contributing factor for determing values. Pieces which have a high degree of availability (especially later wares), should not be as costly as pieces with a lower degree of availability (earlier wares).

Articles (pottery and porcelain) which have Moriage ornamentations are unique in their own right. They are intriguing and aesthetically pleasing. Moriage, like so many other Oriental art forms, has been gaining attention and increasing in both appeal and value over the last few years."

Sprigging is the application of small molded relief decoration to the surface of the item as in Wedgwood's Jasper Ware. This type of decoration is made separately in sprig molds. These relief decorations can be found in the shapes of cameos, portraits, raised figures, medallions and ornamental scrolls and designs. The application of the small molded pieces to the surface of the clay item was hand applied by use of liquid clay or slip. Jasper Ware items are generally found in light blue and sage green colors and are decorated with white sprigged-on-bas-reliefs. Blue Jasper Ware was acheived by the addition of cobalt to the clay and the green color was made by adding both cobalt and iron. The Japanese attempted to copy this classical style of pottery using the established blue and green Jasper Ware background colors. However, on the Nippon items, generally slip trailing was used for the decoration rather than the sprigging technique employed on Jasper Ware. Nippon collectors refer to this type of decor as Nippon Wedgwood and most pieces found today have the blue background with white clay slip trailed on the item. It was an attempt to simulate the classical Wedgwood style.

England's principal contribution to porcelain decoration was the application of the transfer print. It was a relatively simple process, commonly called decalcomania or the transferring of a wet tissue paper thin print to the porcelain surface of an item. It was an inexpensive substitute for hand painted decoration.

This style of decorating made the item look hand painted and it can often be difficult to detect. However, if one looks under a high power magnifying glass, the print appears to have tiny dots making up the design. If the design is the same all over the item, each flower painted exactly alike, chances are it is a decal piece. On some items decals were used for the majority of the design with the artist outlining only with a little trim. Often, the center of a plate or bowl will have transfer work but the border will be hand painted. Most souvenir pieces displaying the Capitol Building in Washington, D.C. are decorated with decals. When used in conjunction with hand painted work the item could then truthfully bear the backstamp of hand painted Nippon as some of it actually had been hand painted. Both the decal and the hand painted touches could be fired at the same time making this a very economical way to produce the wares.

The tapestry texture on Nippon items is similar to that of the Royal Bayreuth pieces. A cloth was first dipped in porcelain slip. The artisan then spread this cloth out on his hands to pat out the excess clay. The material was stretched tightly over the damp piece of porcelain and during the bisque firing the material was consumed. The heat in the kiln destroyed the threads of the material leaving a texture on some items that resembled cheesecloth or linen. Some pieces have a fine-grained appearance, others have a slight pebbly look resembling needlepoint. Many tapestry items appear as though thay had originally been covered with netting, linen, cheesecloth or muslin. Whatever weave the fabric had now became the background texture on the porcelain item. The piece was then painted and fired again. Some Nippon tapestry articles can be found that also have a slip-trailing decor (Moriage) applied over the top of the painted fabric look.

Another type copied by the Japanese was the Gouda ceramics. These wares were originally made in Gouda which is a province of South-Holland. Gouda ceramics tended to copy the Art Nouveau style which featured naturalistic shapes and flowing lines. Art Nouveau wares are named after the French words meaning, new art. The period from 1885 to 1925 is known as the Art Nouveau period and during this time artists attempted to find new styles and break away from the Victorian designs.

Items molded in relief or so-called 'blown-out' pieces have a three dimensional appearance and are very desirable items among collectors. The pattern for this type of item was made directly in the mold. Recesses were cut into the mold producing a negative relief. Whatever was incised into the mold would protrude out on the completed item. The design is raised up from the background of the item and is often in the shape of nuts, flowers, animals, figures, etc. The figures and forms stand out from a flat surface and are raised above the background. The design in relief looks almost as though it had been cut or etched but actually it was pattern-molded. The item was made in one piece. The figures are generally in half relief or semi relief (mezzo-relievo). World Book Encyclopedia describes half relief decoration as being where the ornamentation stands out about half of its thickness and the figures are only partly molded. Some items are in high relief (alto-relievo) where the figures or design project out more than half of their implied thickness while others are found in low relief (bas-relief) where the decoration is just slightly raised and at times may be nearly as flat as that found on a coin.

These items are not actually blown-out as the term tends to indicate, only glass items can be blown, but this is a term used quite commonly by Nippon collectors and dealers to describe this type of work. The pattern gives the appearance of being 'blown-out' or raised as if there had been upward pressure from the underside of the item. These pieces are not to be confused with those that simply have a heavy slip-trailing decoration added on after the item has been molded. There are also items to be found in Nippon porcelain that at first glance appear to be relief molded but are actually decorated with sprigged-on relief ornamentation. The raised part of these items was actually molded separately and attached to the body of the item with porcelain slip. The molded in relief or so-called 'blown-out' pieces are very unique and today command some of the highest prices in Nippon wares. All types are to be found, from placques, tankard sets, vases, ferners, bowls, etc. Placques that seem to be the most desirable are those with figures on them. Popular ones with collectors are those with fishermen, figures in Dutch costume, the Indian portrait, Indian on horseback, and the Egyptian desert scene with riders and camels. Others in demand have horses, stag in the forest, a moose, and the lion and lioness. Tankard sets are extremely rare and the only style I have ever seen has a scene of a deer in the forest. Vases are generally found with flowers, fruits or figures. The designs in the molded relief patterns are varied and new ones are constantly being found by collectors.

Porcelain cloisonné imitates other Oriental cloisonné pieces except that it is produced on a **porcelain body** rather than metal. Most cloisonné pieces are formed of wire, copper, brass, etc. which was attached to a **metal body** by either soldering or glue. The decoration was divided into cells or so-called cloisons. The cloisons were separated by these strips of soft metal and filled with enamel which fused to the body upon firing. The wire kept the colors separated and often outlined fruits, flowers, butterflies, animals, human figures, leaves, birds, dragons and arabesque designs. On the Nippon porcelain cloisonné, the enameling often resembles set stones while some appear to have a cork-like substance inlaid, somewhat resembling tree bark. Nippon marked pieces are extremely difficult to find!

Beading is a type of decoration which is used on many pieces of Nippon. It generally consists of a series of dots of clay slip which were painted in a number of colors, although gold and brown beading seem to be very popular on items. Very often the dots will be of the same size on a piece while others will have several sizes applied. When gold was painted on, it had to be fired at lower temperatures than that used for other decoration, otherwise the gold would sink into the enamel and disappear into the glazed decoration. On later Nippon pieces much of the beading was done merely with the artist's brush, very quickly, with a splash of enameling. Many pieces found with this decor were made to resemble jewels, rubies, emeralds, etc.

Some of the other designs and techniques used on Nippon wares are items featuring a Dutch motif (windmills, figures in Dutch costume), Russian dancers, Roman ruins, the woodland scene, Chinese designs and geometrical patterns such as those used by Egyptian potters over 3000 years ago. (See examples next page). Certain scenes are prized by collectors for their rarity.

American Indian designs are among the more difficult to find. The designs that seem to be portrayed the most frequently are those of the Indian in a canoe on a lake, Indian teepees on a river, the Indian warrior, Indian on horseback, the Indian hunting wild game and the Indian on a white horse. Research indicates that a series of Indian portraits was manufactured, each representing different tribes and each is shown in full head dress.

Art Nouveau styled pieces were also popular during the Nippon era. This period in history when the Art Nouveau style was most popular was from 1885-1925. It was a time when realism was rejected by the artists and bolder colors were used. It was a period of 'new style'. Free flowing designs and many naturalistic floral patterns were used. Commonly found patterns have tendril-like forms, sweeping and flowing lines, elongated figures and flowers and leaves. Many of the Art Nouveau maidens were portrayed with long flowing hair. It was a time when the artists wanted to break away from the imitations of the past.

Some Nippon pieces were designed with an Art Deco style decoration. This style hit its peak in 1925 but did appear on items manufactured as early as 1910-1915. The items had a modernistic style, many with geometric designs. Motifs commonly used were shapes such as circles, rectangles, cylinders and cones.

The Azalea pattern so popular today with Noritake collectors was also produced with a Nippon backstamp during the last few years of the Nippon period. The Larkin Company offered Azalea patterned china items to its customers as premiums when they purchased the Larkin products. An old ad for the Larkin Co. states "Purchases of these Larkin products bring lovely premiums. Beauty! Charm! Richness! All these are found in this lovely pattern. No wonder it is popular! It is just as lovely as it looks-dainty and thin and wonderfully hand-painted". The Larkin Co. was established in 1875 in Buffalo, N.Y. by John D. Larkin. Sweet Home Soap was one of their most famous products. In later years the company diversified and eventually sold tea, coffee, extracts, varnishes, paints, furniture, garments, etc. and even baking goods. The Larkin Club Plan was a big promotion with the company. It was handled through the mail and was devised so that housewives could purchase Larkin products and receive valuable premiums as well. Each group had a secretary and every member paid a dollar or two each month towards their purchases. The secretary received additional premiums for her efforts. It was a tremendous success and helped to eliminate the middleman. The Larkin Co. preferred to pass on the extra savings from not hiring salesmen to the customers in the way of premiums.

The Larkin Co. gave many different kinds of china as premiums over the years. The 1901 Larkin catalog displays Buffalo Pottery which helped to contribute to the growth of the Buffalo Pottery Company. The ad states "By trade agreement, American Potters sell "seconds" for use as premiums, but every piece of our Buffalo Pottery ware is strictly the first selection of the finest crockery in America".

When the United States entered World War I the military increased their orders of Buffalo Pottery and these products were then dropped from the Larkin catalog for the term of the war. In order to fill the orders much china ware was imported from other countries. Since Japan was a major producer of porcelain the Noritake Company was commissioned to fill many of the Larkin orders. Their ad stated that, "The Azalea pattern was exclusive with the Larkin Company".

The majority of Azalea pieces found today have the Noritake backstamp on them but to date I have found this pattern on Nippon marked items but only with three Nippon marks, the blue rising sun, the blue maple leaf and the magenta M in wreath. No doubt it was also made having other Nippon marks.

One could build a whole dinner set, piece by piece. The hand painted Noritake pattern is one of pink azaleas with green to gray leaves and gold rims. Azalea flowers are funnel shaped and are found in abundance in the hilly regions in Asia, so it is natural for the Japanese to paint this particular design. The Nippon pieces appear to match

Basket Weave
Design

the Noritake marked ones except that their colors seem to be a bit more muted. The Nippon tea cups, however, are a little larger in size but when the two are mixed together it is difficult to tell one from the other. The Azalea pattern is a fast growing collectible item and the Nippon pieces are the most desirable. First, because of their Azalea design and second because they are the earlier pieces of porcelain.

The Japanese employed so many techniques on the Nippon wares. There are items which have had the design incised right into the body. This process was accomplished when the article was still in a state of soft clay and a sharp tool or stick was used to produce the design. I also have a very unique vase on which the pattern was stamped on. The stamping process is different from incising as it generally results in an impressed decoration of a repeated pattern. Again soft clay was necessary and the design was pressed into the clay with either a special tool or an item such as a button. The design on many of these items could also have been cut into a plaster roller. This was rolled over the item and the design emerged in relief.

Portrait pieces are very much in demand with collectors and many are paintings of Victorian ladies. Some others featured are Queen Louise, Countess Anna Potocka and Lebrun. Madame Vigel Lebrun (1755-1842) was a French artist who was a favorite of Marie Antoinette. Portrait items were very fashionable to have in the home in the Victorian era. Today, they are fairly hard to find and the price has naturally gone upward with the demand. Some of the items appear to be hand painted while others are definitely decal work.

Artist signed pieces are also collector items and always seeem to fetch higher prices. Signatures enhance items but never guarantee quality. It is always interesting to note if the signature is one of Japanese extraction or of another nationality. Most pieces painted in Nippon were not signed by the artists as the Japanese seemed to prefer to remain anonymous with their works of art. I do have one item signed Kimu which sounds as if it could be a Japanese name. Probably most of the signed pieces were painted during the heyday of hand painting china ware either here in the United States or in England as most signatures do appear to be English names.

Some pieces of Nippon can be found having a marbleized effect for part or all of the design. A myriad of colors were used and irregular swirling lines make up the pattern.

Gold and silver overlay pieces are very desirable and among the higher priced Nippon pieces. Some have heavy gold or silver on a cobalt background, some on white porcelain, some on floral or scenic designs. Both the gold and silver colors had to be fired separately at lower temperatures than the others so that the colors would not melt and sink into the enamel decoration. Discoloration of the color occurred when the items were overfired and silver even turned black in color. Many of the items with silver trim tarnish, however, when the silver was mixed with platinum it did not. Since silver melts at an even lower temperature than gold, the platinum was originally added to raise the melting point. It was then discovered that this combination worked out better than plain silver.

Cobalt items were made with oxidized cobalt blue coloring. Originally, in Japan, gosu, a pebble found in Oriental riverbeds had been used for the cobalt coloring of items. This was a natural cobalt but quite scarce and expensive to use. In the late 1860's oxidized cobalt was imported into Japan and used in its place. Cobalt oxide is the most powerful of all the coloring oxides for tinting. Many cobalt items have a heavy overlay of gold or tend to be scenic or floral pieces.

Coralene beading is a very unique form of decorating an item. Tiny colored or transparent glass beads were originally applied to glass items in the shapes of birds, flowers, leaves, etc. The most popular design used was one which resembled seaweed or **coral**, hence the name **coralene** was given to it. The articles often had thousands of beads fired on, giving the items a plush velvety look. Japanese coralene was patened in 1909 by Alban L. Rock, an American living in Yokohama, Japan. Most of these pieces are signed Kinran, US Patent, NBR 912171, February 9, 1909, Japan. No doubt these porcelain items were an attempt to copy the technique used on glass. Articles decorated in this manner and backstamped Nippon are difficult to find.

Sometsuke style items were decorated with an underglaze of blue and white colors and some Nippon wares can be found decorated in this mannner. Many bear the backstamp of Royal Sometuke which has a slightly different spelling. Many of these pieces have the phoenix bird pattern painted on them. (See Page 25)

Cartoon and comical items are also popular. They again seem harder to find but some items can even be found bearing cartoon figures including Jiggs of the Maggie and Jiggs comic strip characters. Novelties such as figurines seem to be among the rarer items and collecting Nippon dolls can be a whole hobby in itself.

Dolls tend to remind us of our childhood and many were manufactured which were never intended to be children's playthings. Nippon dolls come in a variety of sizes and styles and some of the very small all bisque dolls were originally used for play in the dollhouse. The Japanese word for doll is ningyō meaning human being and image. Porcelain dolls are not really authentic Japanese dolls but merely imitations of foreign dolls. The solid bisque bodies were popular from 1880 into the twentieth century and the Japanese copied all the European designs. Kyoto became the center in Japan for making porcelain dolls. Germany had previously been the leader in the field of doll making but at the outbreak of World War I trade with most countries was halted. Japan then stepped up production and became the new leader in the field for a number of years. Some dolls have painted hair, some have wigs, some have solid porcelain bodies, some are jointed, while others have cloth or composition bodies. Nippon boy dolls are harder to find which is reflected in their price. Some Nippon dolls have the Morimura Brothers mark incised on them, many are simply incised with the word Nippon. The mark is usually found on the back of the doll's shoulders or head, however some even have the mark on the bottom of the feet. There are small standing character dolls which were made with molded hair and molded clothing, some are even portrayed in sailor suits, Buster Brown suits, etc. Queue San Baby is a small bisque doll which has jointed arms and slippers and cap and queue (a long braid down its back). It also had a sticker on its chest giving its name. Some of the very small bisque dolls were even used on birthday cakes as decorations.

Two of the favorites with collectors are the all bisque Kewpies and Happifats. A patent was first obtained for the Kewpie doll in 1913 by Rose O'Neill and today some Nippon ones may still be found bearing the original Rose O'Neill Copyright 1913 sticker on them. As with all Kewpie collectibles the price is generally higher than for other dolls the same size.

The charming Happifats have little rounded bodies and were originally manufactured by the Borgfeldt Co. Later imitations were made by the Japanese and they are dressed in molded suits and dresses.

Morimura Bros. began selling bisque head dolls as early as 1915. The 'Dolly' doll was designed by Frederick Langfelder who was granted a patent for it in 1917. He then turned it over to Morimura Bros. for manufacture and distribution. This doll had a molded bathing suit on and originally came with a diamond shaped red and gold paper label on its stomach with the word 'Dolly'. The word Nippon was incised on the back of the doll's shoulders.

Morimura Bros. also had another trademark on the 'Baby Darling' doll. This doll is all bisque with jointed arms. She has molded hair with a ribbon in it. The word Nippon is incised on the back of her shoulders and a sticker was placed on her stomach saying 'Baby Darling' plus the initials MB which stood for Morimura Bros. Today it is rare to find these dolls with the original sticker still intact. Morimura Bros. was a leader in this country for importing Nippon dolls and some of the dolls they sold were 'Baby Ella', 'Baby Rose', 'Baby O'Mine'. In 1920 they even advertised French glass eyes on their dolls and also had an office in Canada as well as the United States.

Some other companies I have been able to locate that imported Nippon dolls into the United States are E.I. Horsman Co.; Horsman and Aetna Dolls Co.; Nagai and Co., New York City; Fould and Freure, NYC; Haber Bros., NYC; Geo. Borgfeldt and Co.; Louis Wolf and Co., Boston Mass. and NYC; Tajimi Co., Chicago; Taijo Trading Co., NYC and Toronto; and Son Bros., San Francisco, California.

Many of the dolls were named and research indicates there was a Nippon 'Jollikid' doll, 'Wide-a wake', 'Chubby', 'Baby Lucy' and 'Best Baby' which looked like a Kewpie doll.

Japanese Symbols, Crests and Mons

Japan is a country of great natural beauty. The Japanese people have a love for simplified beauty. They also love flowers and nature and represent them in all of their works of art. Flowers have become almost a cult in Japan. The Japanese prefer flowering cherry trees in spring and autumn colored flowers for fall rather then the bold and exotic colored ones. The cherry tree is cultivated in Japan specifically for its blossoms and not for the fruit. The cherry blossom is the national flower of the country and also the emblem of the faithful warrior. The peony is a symbol of summer and is considered the king of flowers. The orchid stands for hidden beauty and modesty. The iris flowers are beloved by the Japanese as they feel the iris wards off evil spirits and is a charm used against illness. The iris is also said to evoke the warm days of summer in the artist. This flower was associated with warriors because of the sword-like leaves. In fact, the Japanese celebrated the fifth day of the fifth month as the Iris Fete. It was called Boy's Day, now called Children's Day and was set aside to honor the sons in a family. The carp symbolized strength and perserverance and carp banners (fish shaped flags) are flown on this day.

The daffodil represents spring and the water lily is for autumn. Both the narcissus plant and fern leaves stand for good fortune. The chrysanthamum stands for good health and longevity because it blooms late in the year and lives longer than other flowers. It is also the crest of the Emperor of Japan, kiku no mon. The paulownia flowers and leaves are the crest of the Empress of Japan, kiri no mon.

Crests are family symbols known as mon in Japanese. The subjects range from flowers, animals, fruits, and the designs are unlimited.

Ernest Lehner has published a book entitled *Symbols, Signs and Signets* by Dover Publishing, Inc., NYC, 1969. In that book he lists many Japanese crests, ten of which I have permission to reprint. (See Page 24)

> #829 Standard Bearer by Totoya Hakkei (1780-1850)
> #830 Kikumon, chrysanthemum crest of the Emperor
> #831 Kirimon, Paulownia Imperialis Crest of the Empress
> #834 Dragon crest
> #842 Iris
> #845 Tree peony
> #846 Cherry blossom
> #848 Plum blossom
> #851 Wood sorrel
> #852 Grapes

The Japanese also feel that every tree has a spirit which is part of the life of the tree. The bamboo, pine and apricot trees are all good-luck symbols. The plum stands for womanhood. The pine tree is a sign of winter, it also represents strength, friendship and prosperity and pine needles are often used by the Japanese artists in their designs. The bamboo is a symbol of strength, straight and unbending. It resists the storm but yields to it and rises again.

Peacocks stand for elegance and good fortune and are often found together in design with the peony flower. The deer stood for divine messenger. The crane means good luck and longevity and the tiger (tora) is a symbol of strength and safety. The tortoise is a symbol of longevity and large stones and rocks stand for power and strength.

The Japanese treat many subjects in symbolic form using mons or crests in their designs. Mythological creatures also play a great part in the art work of Japan. The dragon is considered a symbol of strength, goodness and good fortune. Dragons are the most highly esteemed of all mythical beasts to the Japanese and are believed to reside in the sky. The Japanese dragon has three claws as opposed to the Chinese dragon which has five. Paintings of them are often accompanied by either lightening, clouds, water or flame symbols and the dragon is frequently portrayed in a relief style decor utilizing the slip trailing method (Moriage). Research indicates that items portraying the raised relief dragon with a gray background date back no earlier than 1918. Items portraying the dragon in this Moriage style were for export only and are still being manufactured in Japan.

The phoenix bird, also referred to as the Hō-ō bird, or ho-ho bird, is sort of a bird of paradise who resides on earth and is associated with the Empress of Japan. It is also a symbol to the Japanese of all that is beautiful. This bird often appears to be a cross between a peacock, a pheasant, and a gamecock. There seem to be many designs for this bird as each artist had his own conception as to how it should look. (See Page 25)

* The long mark over a vowel means that it is pronounced twice as long, o sounds like oo.

Japanese Crests

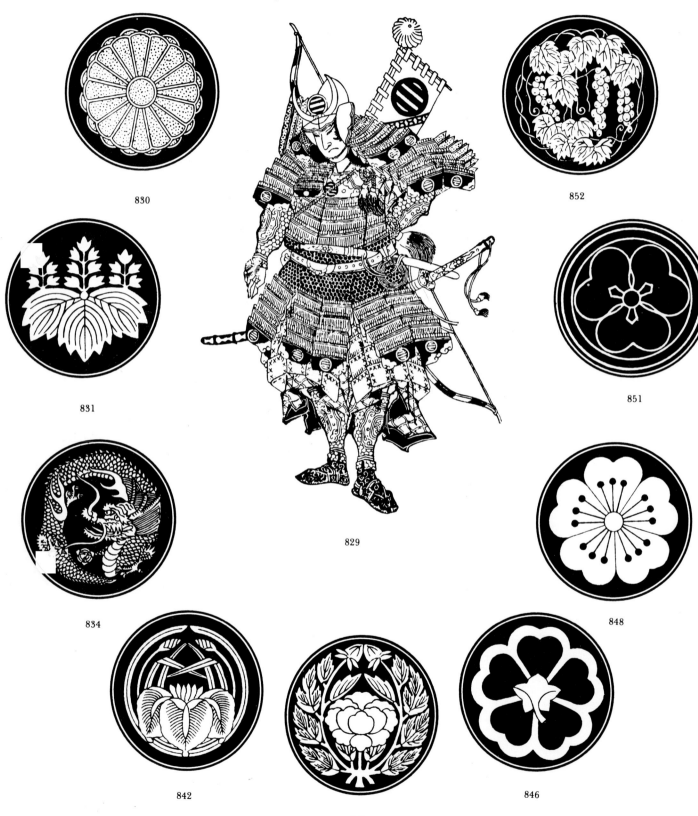

830

852

831

851

829

834

848

842

845

846

Examples of phoenix bird designs found on Nippon porcelain

Marking System

As stated earlier in the book, the McKinley Tariff Act was passed in 1890 to give more protection for United States manufacturers. Among other things it stated the following:

> Chapter 1244, Section 6 "That on and after the first day of March, eighteen hundred and ninety-one, all articles of foreign manufacture, such as are usually or ordinarily marked, stamped, branded or labeled , and all packages containing such or other imported articles, shall, respectively, be plainly marked, stamped, branded or labeled in legible English words, so as to indicate the country of their origin; and unless so marked, stamped, branded or labeled they shall not be admitted to entry".

On December 20, 1890 a circular was issued to Officers of the Customs and others concerned: "While the question as to whether goods imported on and after March 1, 1891, are properly "marked, stamped, branded or labeled" under the above provision is to be decided by collectors of customs at the time of importation, and the language of the section is so plain as to hardly require an interpretation by the Department, yet, in view of the great number of inquiries received from importers and others, it is deemed proper to publish some of the conclusions reached by the Department in the premises for the information of all concerned.

1. While only such goods or articles of foreign manufacture "as are usually or ordinarily marked, stamped, branded or labeled" are required to be so marked, etc., on and after the first of March, 1891, yet it will be observed that **all packages, outside or other,** containing any imported merchandise **must be so marked,** etc., to entitle the contents thereof to entry at the custom-house.

3. In the case of small articles which can not be readily marked, the marking of the inside cartons and outside packages will be sufficient.

6. The prefix "from" placed before the name of the country of origin as, for instance, "from France," "from Germany," etc., is not essential, the law requiring simply the name of the country of origin to appear.

14. Articles and packages may be marked either by stamping, branding or labeling, as the party may choose.

15. In the case of pencils, steel pens, tooth brushes, licorice stick, common crockery, etc., the law will be complied with if the cartons and packages containing the same are marked.

18. The law **does not require the name of the importer, shipper or maker,** to be marked, stamped, etc., on imported articles or packages."

A Customs regulation persuant to The Tariff Act of 1890 was issued in 1892 stating the following:

> ART. 311. All imported articles which are usually marked, stamped, branded or labeled, and all packages containing imported goods, shall be plainly marked in English words to indicate the country of origin, otherwise they shall be excluded from entry. Collectors must decide whether imported goods conform to these requirements, under the following rules: The country of origin, and not the locality of manufacture, must be shown, and abbreviations which are sufficiently definite may be accepted. In the case of articles which are usually packed in cartons or bands it will suffice if the inside and outside packages are marked with the name of the country of origin. The marking of goods after importation is not a compliance with the law. Articles usually imported in bulk, when secured together for convenience in handling, are not considered packages requiring to be marked. Merchandise intended for immediate export or for transit to Mexico or Canada does not come within the scope of the laws as to marking, stamping, branding, etc."

A Treasury Act of 1894, Chapter 349, Section 5 stated:

> "That all articles of foreign manufacture, such as are usually or ordinarily marked, stamped, branded or labeled, and all packages containing such or other imported articles, shall, respectively, be plainly marked, stamped, branded or labeled in legible English words, so as to indicate the country of their origin and the quantity of their contents; and until so marked, stamped, branded or labeled they shall not be delivered to the importer should any article of imported merchandise be marked, stamped, branded or labeled so as to indicate a quantity, number or measurement in excess of the quantity, number, or measurement actually contained in such article, no delivery of the same shall be made to the importer until the mark, stamp, brand or label, as the case may be, shall be changed so as to confirm to the facts of the case."

The Tariff Act of 10/3/13, subsection 1, paragraph F of Section 4 states:

> "That all articles of foreign manufacture or production which are capable of being marked, stamped, branded or labeled, **without injury,** shall be marked, stamped, branded or labeled in legible English words, **in a conspicuous place that shall not be covered or obscured by any subsequent attachments or arrangements,** so as to indicate the country of origin. Said marking, stamping, branding or labeling shall be as **nearly indelible and permanent as the nature of the article will permit."**

Treasury Decision 34740 of August 31, 1914 stated:

> (T.D. 34740.)
>
> *Marking of Japanese articles.*
>
> Articles produced in Japan and marked with the word "Nippon" legally marked under
> subsection 1 of paragraph F of section 4 of the tariff act of 1913.
>
> TREASURY DEPARTMENT, *August 31, 1914.*

Sir: The department refers to your letter of the 24th ultimo, in relation to an inquiry from a customs broker at your port whether brushes manufactured in Japan and marked with the word "Nippon" would be considered as legally marked under subsection 1 of paragraph F of section 4 of the tariff act of October 3, 1913, which requires all articles of foreign production, capable of being marked, to be marked in legible English words so as to indicate the country of origin.

The reports received by the department indicate that there is a variance in practice at the several ports in regard to the admission of Japanese articles bearing the word "Nippon." While it appears that the word "Nippon" is the Japanese name for Japan, it is so commonly employed in this country to designate Japan that it may now be considered as incorporated in our language with a well-established meaning.

The department is therefore of the opinion that articles produced in Japan and marked with the word "Nippon" are legally marked under subsection 1 of paragraph F. The inquiry of the broker should therefore be answered in the affirmative.

Respectfully,   ANDREW J. PETERS,
(68174-11.)   *Assistant Secretary,*
COLLECTOR OF CUSTOMS, *San Francisco, Cal.*

(T.D. 36989.)
Marking Chinaware.

Chinaware and porcelain not marked to indicate the country of origin at the time of importation may be released when marked by means of a gummed label or with a rubber stamp.

TREASURY DEPARTMENT, *February 8, 1917.*

SIR: The department refers to your letter of the 17th ultimo, reporting on a communication of various importers of Japanese and Chinese earthenware and porcelain in regard to the marking of such merchandise to indicate the country of origin under the provisions of subsection 1 of paragraph F of section 4 of the existing tariff act.

It appears that it is the practice at your port for the appraiser to pass Chinese goods bought in the open market without any marking to indicate the country of origin and to require Japanese goods of the same character to be marked with a pasted label or with a rubber stamp. It appears that substantially the same practice exists at most of the larger ports, and that **unless the merchandise is manufactured especially for the American trade permanent marking is not required.**

In this connection attention is invited to T.D. 36970, wherein the department held that articles capable of being marked without injury in their condition as imported must be so marked prior to their release from customs custody and that such marking must be as nearly permanent and indelible as the nature of the article will permit.

As the appraiser expresses the opinion that it **would be commercially impracticable to mark indelibly chinaware and porcelain in its condition as imported, such merchandise not marked at the time of importation to indicate the country of origin may be released when marked by means of a gummed label or with a rubber stamp.**

Respectfully,   ANDREW J. PETERS
(68174-2.)   *Assistant Secretary.*
COLLECTOR OF CUSTOMS, New York.

(T.D. 38643.)
Marking of Japanese imports.

Marking of Japanese merchandise with the word "Nippon" not a compliance with the law — T.D.
34740 and T.D. 37828 revoked, effective six months from date.

TREASURY DEPARTMENT, *March 1, 1921.*
To collectors of customs and others concerned:

Reference is made to the provisions of T.D. 34740 of August 31, 1914, and T.D. 37828 of December 9, 1918, by authority of which merchandise imported from Japan and marked with the name "Nippon" is admitted to entry as conforming, respectively, to *(a)* paragraph F, subsection 1, section IV, of the tariff act of 1913, which requires imported merchandise to be marked to indicate the country of origin in the manner therein described *in legible English words, and (b)* the provisos to paragraphs 128 and 130 of the said act, which require merchandise of the character therein described to be marked with the *name* of the country of origin.

T.D 34740 proceeds upon the theory that the word "Nippon" is so commonly employed in this country to designate Japan that it may be considered as incorporated into the English language; and T.D. 37828 on the principle that "Nippon" is in fact the name of Japan.

Renewed consideration has been given to the question of the legality of the marking authorized in the above-cited decisions; and **after examination into the history and derivation of the word "Nippon" and its treatment by lexicographers of recognized standing, the department is constrained to the conclusion that "Nippon" is a Japanese word, the English equivalent of which is "Japan,"** and that the weight of authority does not support the earlier view that the word has become incorporated into the English language.

The department is of the opinion, therefore, that the requirement of paragraph F, supra, with respect to marking in legible English words, is not satisfied by the use of the word "Nippon" **and you are instructed that merchandise from Japan, the marking of which is governed by this provision of law, should not be released when bearing only the Japanese word "Nippon" to indicate Japan.**

The provisos to paragraphs 128 and 130, supra, while requiring that imported articles of the character therein enumerated shall be marked with the name of the country of origin, do not specifically state that such marking shall be in English words, but a consideration of the general purpose of the marking laws, namely to inform all users as to the origin of imported merchandise, and of further fact that it was the obvious intent of Congress in enacting these special statutes, to require greater precision in the marking of the merchandise therein provided for than is imposed by the general marking statute, leads irresistibly to the conclusion that "the name of the country of origin" con-

templated is the English name thereof, and not a foreign name, which would convey no meaning to large numbers of users of the merchandise in this country.

You are further instructed, therefore, that imports from Japan falling within the provisions of the said paragraphs 128 and 130 should not be permitted delivery unless marked with the English name of the country of origin, as well as the name of the maker or purchaser.

You are also instructed to apply the principle of this ruling to Japanese imports coming within the purview of paragraph 161 of the tariff act.

T.D. 34740 and T.D. 37828 are, therefore hereby revoked, such provocation and the new practice herein outlined to become effective six months from the date hereof.

ANGUS W. McLEAN, *Assistant Secretary.*

I have included most sections of the law that I could find regarding the marking of Nippon porcelain items in the United States. There is a lot to digest and at times it is a bit confusing but I felt that it should all finally be added in a book. I also corresponded with the Patent Office, Trade Marks Registry, 25 Southampton Buildings, London, with regard to their import marking requirements. They sent the following information:

"A trade mark is a means of identification. It is a symbol (whether word, device or a combination of the two) which a person uses in the course of trade in order that his goods may be readily distinguished by the purchasing public from similar goods of other traders. Registration of a trade mark confers a statutory monopoly in the use of that mark in relation to the goods for which it is registered, and the registered owner has the right to sue in the Courts for infringement of his mark".

The Registrar went on to say "As far as origin marking of porcelain in concerned, under the Merchandise Marks Act, 1926, imported goods bearing the name or trade mark of a British manufacturer or trader could not be sold unless accompanied by an indication of origin. The relevant statutory instrument marking order is SR & O 1928 No 570 as amended by SR & 1939 No 393. A photocopy is attached. **No earlier references to the origin marking of porcelain have been found.**"

BUTTERWORTHS ANNOTATED LEGISLATION SERVICE
NO. 83.—MERCHANDISE MARKS

PART I
(IMPORTATION AND SALE)

The undermentioned goods are required to bear an indication of origin (1) at the time of importation and also (2) at the time of sale wholesale and by retail, and of exposure for sale wholesale and by retail (including exposure for sale wholesale by a person being a wholesale dealer).

POTTERY

(S.R. & O. 1928 No. 570, as amended by S.R. & O. 1939 No. 393)

Pottery of the following descriptions:

(*a*) The following articles of china or translucent pottery (including pottery known as china or porcelain), general earthenware or semi-porcelain (excluding terra-cotta ware, stone ware, and red and brown pottery), jet, rocking-ham or samian—

(i) articles commonly used in connection with the serving of food or drink;
(ii) kitchen ware and utensils;
(iii) bedroom and other toilet ware;
(iv) heraldic and souvenir ware, including ware bearing any heraldic or similar device or any motto or monogram or any picture of a place in the United Kingdom or any phrase in the English language:

(*b*)(i) Floor tiles for tesselated pave-ments;
(ii) glazed wall and hearth tiles;
(*c*)(i) Sanitary earthenware, white, and cane and white;
(ii) enameled sanitary ware of fireclay;
(iii) other sanitary ware (not including drain pipes).

NOTES—(1) The requirements do not apply to any article (not being heraldic or souvenir ware) which is

(i) an object of art, whether antique or not, wholly or mainly for ornamental use;
(ii) a toy;
(iii) a subsidiary part of a composite article in which the pottery is united with other material;
(iv) pottery for mounting, i.e. pottery made for the purpose of being united with other material so as to form a

composite article.

(2) Where a lid or cover accompanies a pot, bowl, or dish, the lid or cover need not be marked where the pot, bowl, or dish itself bears an indication of origin.

(3) Where pottery of the following description: —

(a) sanitary earthenware, white or cane and white;
(b) enameled sanitary ware of fireclay;
(c) other sanitary ware (not including drain pipes)

is exposed for sale under conditions which do not afford reasonable facility to prospective purchasers for the inspection of the indication of origin borne, in accordance with the provisions of the Order at the time of importation, the indication of origin on exposure for sale shall be borne on an adhesive label securely affixed to the article.

As required and in compliance with the American Customs regulations effective 3/1/91, the word Nippon was backstamped on most items exported from Japan to this country until 1921. However, we don't usually find the word Nippon all by itself. It is generally used in conjunction with many different markings, some symbols (which both the Japanese and English speaking people could both understand), and some writing. Deciphering these marks can be quite difficult at times. Just what do all these marks mean to us? Some people feel that they are quite useless but I think that the study of these marks can be quite fascinating. It is true that the quality of workmanship on items varies within the same mark, however, they can be collected for their own sake. Every mark has to have a history behind it and it can be a challenge trying to find out more about them or speculating on just why the item is marked as it is. From all available information I can gather, in addition to the word Nippon the backstamp may contain the name of the kiln, the potter, a symbol representing a family name, names of towns, sections or provinces of Japan, marks of agents, family concerns manufacturing the wares, or exporter or importer marks.

The marks may be stamped on, incised into the item, put on with a paper sticker or gummed label, or even be a rubber stamp mark (as of 1917). However, I still tend to be leary of buying items with stickers and labels as it is always possible to put a fake mark on an item. Much to our disappointment early potters had no idea that their work would someday be collected and that identification would be important to the collector.

There were even a number of small studios in the United States during the early part of the 1900's which specialized in hand painting of china ware 'in the white blanks' imported from other countries. Hand painting of china was a popular pastime in both the United States and England and it became quite fashionable among the ladies during the late 19th and early 20th century. China painting first became popular in England and then spread to the United States. During this late Victorian era many people set up business and taught this fine and genteel art. Women flocked to these establishments and could select from hundreds of pieces of undecorated china to paint. Large decorating firms were also started in the cities and they imported 'in the white' china from manufacturers around the world. Foreign china was considered more desirable than that made in America. Two techniques were employed for decorating the wares:

    1. Overglaze technique, where the painting was applied to an item which already had a fired glazed surface. This item was then refired to make the china painting permanent.

    2. Underglaze technique, done on bisque china, then glazed and fired.

In the listing of identifying marks on the following pages you will note such marks as Spicer Studios, Akron, Ohio and the Pickard china mark, representative of the Pickard decorating studio originally located in Chicago. I wrote to the Pickard China Co. regarding these pieces and was given the following information, "At the turn of the century Wilder A. Pickard founded a china decorating studio in Chicago. He specialized in hand painted art pieces and dessert and tea sets. Most of the original artists were from Chicago's famous Art Institute. Business mounted swiftly. Soon the staff was swelled by renowned ceramic artists from all the countries of Europe. Since most china was manufactured abroad at that time, the Pickard studios imported blank ware to be decorated. These early hand painted pieces are now sought after by collectors. Later, production was moved to Antioch, in the lovely lake region of northern Illinois. Although the company's sales now are primarily in fine china dinnerware, Pickard still manufactures a line of decorative accessories introduced by Wilder Pickard in 1915, with 23 karat gold hand-painted over an intricate rose and daisy design in etched relief." The Pickard Co. also decorated Japanese wares in other patterns. One pattern was called Bouquet Satsuma. It was high relief enamel on Satsuma ware. These wares were made by the Royal Potteries near Kagoshina, Japan founded in 1539 by Prince Chiusa. The dishes feature a fine crackle in the glaze and Chinese flowers painted on in brilliant enamels. On many of the Pickard decorated Nippon pieces there was a design of etching with two coats of purest gold applied. One Nippon/Pickard piece that I own is signed A. Richter. Research indicates that this was Adolph Richter, a man of German origin, who specialized in stylized designs. He was one of the top artists of the Ravenswood period 1905-1919. The Ravenswood studio was located in a north central section of Chicago. A signature greatly enhances the value of a Pickard item as well as Nippon items.

Many pieces of Nippon porcelain found today were originally sold as souvenirs and fairings or given away as advertising items. Fairings are items which were either won or bought at fairs as a souvenir of the event. Collectors find commemorative items to be of special interest as they are also valued for their historical significance.

Businesses could order items with their name on them or perhaps place a paper sticker with their advertisement on them. They were generally given away as gifts to customers. These items tend to be more difficult to find and I am always excited and intrigued when I come across one. An ink blotter in my collection has a green M in wreath for its backstamp and the original paper sticker bearing the words "Compliments of Morimura Bros. 1913". Morimura Bros. opened in NYC in 1876 and imported Japanese wares into this country until 1941. This blotter was probably once part of a desk set given away by the importer, perhaps to agents or buyers placing large orders. Other Nippon advertising items I have seen are marked "Compliments of Eastern Outfitting Co.".

I do find that many of the advertising and souvenir items are not of the finest quality porcelain and possibly this is why some collectors shy away from them. It has been my experience though that the purchase of one invariably leads to another. They are an interesting collectible and I have managed to acquire an item marked '1919 Toronto Exhibition' and a small dish backstamped '1912 Fair, D.M. Read Co., Bridgeport, Conn.' Other items to be found are souvenirs of resorts, Newport, R.I., Portland, Me., etc. Among the most common to be found are those depicting the Capitol Building in Washington, D.C. as it appeared at the turn of the century. All the pieces I have ever seen with this decor, however, have been decorated with a transfer print or so-called decalcomania. Many of these unusual pieces have sent me scurrying off to the library in search of old pictures of the Capitol, for information about the Toronto Exhibition, different fairs and resort areas. At times it has been fruitful and other times it has been to no avail. There seems to be so much to learn.

Items stamped with just the word Nippon or Nippon/Noritake on them generally were 'in the white' blanks decorated elsewhere. Just because the mark says Nippon does not mean that the item was painted there. Many countries imported these blanks. Backstamps with letters and initials seem to be those of the importers in the United States and Canada. There were many companies in the United States importing these wares during the years of 1891-1921. Besides the Pickard Co., these were the Louis Wolf and Co., NYC & Boston, the Spicer Studios in Akron, Ohio, the Jonroth Studios, and Yamato Importing Co., in Chicago to mention a few. The Noritake Co. exported many wares marked with their name and the Okura Art China Co., a branch of the Noritake Co. exported items with their OAC mark.

I have found that two of the Nippon marks seem to be in greater abundance than the others, they are the M in the wreath and the maple leaf. Many marks are identical only they are found in different colors with green, blue and magenta being the most prevalent. Others I have found are tourquoise, brown, orange, gold and black. Some collectors feel that those stamped in green and blue marks seem to be of a higher quality porcelain but perhaps this is just a coincidence.

There are several theories regarding the different colors of marks used. One is that they stand for years of production and the green marks were placed on items during the last years Nippon was produced. Another is that different colors indicated the quality of the porcelain, first quality, green; second, blue and third, magenta colored marks were placed on utility type items. Upon close study there seems to be a number of exceptions to both, so perhaps all I can presently do is record the marks in the hope that someday the mystery will be solved.

Deciphering the marks is difficult at times and exact dating of the items is an almost impossible task. A few articles however, can be easily dated such as the commerative items. The Pickard Co. decorated pieces can also be researched and dated.

The section containing hand drawn facsimiles of identifying marks includes marks found on Nippon porcelain items whether they were decorated in Japan or elsewhere. Articles that have a Nippon mark plus 'Japan' printed on them were evidently manufactured during the transition period around the early 1920's when it was mandatory to add the word Japan.

I have also found Nippon items that had patent numbers printed on them along with the Nippon mark. On the Japanese coralene items, the patent number was issued in the United States so I wrote to the Patent Office in Washington regarding the two I had. One was #30441 which turned out to be a picker staff motion of looms, Oct. 16, 1869, the other #70018 was for a skirt wire on Oct. 22, 1867. England, too, has no record of these patent marks so to date it remains a mystery. They may be of Japanese origin.

Sandra Andacht, author and columnist on Orientalia advises me that when the Noritake Company was first started it was registered as Nippon Gomei Kaisha which means a family owned company with no outside stockholders. In 1917 the name was changed to Nippon Toki Kabushiki Kaisha which means stock was bought by outsiders. From 1904 to 1917, Nippon Toki was used but the word Nippon appears as part of the backstamp (in other words Nippon would appear twice, once in the name and again for country of origin in accordance with US regulations). From 1918, the word Noritake appeared also in conjunction with the word Nippon. The words Nippon Toki and Nippon Kaisha are interchangeable. Pieces are still being manufactured today bearing the name Nippon Toki Noritake.

Many pieces can be found where the item is unmistakably Nippon but not marked so. I personally prefer marked pieces as I feel they have considerably more resale value, however, there are many reasons why they might not be marked. I am certainly not encouraging anyone to go out and start buying unmarked items as it can sometimes be difficult knowing when a piece is authentic. I am merely stating that they do exist and that there are many of them out there. Our Custom laws left many loopholes regarding the original marking of these items, some may have had a decal marking or label on them and it has worn off with time. Others may have been part of a set where only one item was stamped; in time one may have become broken or the pair split up and one is thus left without any mark or identification. Also, during the second World War, sentiment ran high against Japan and many people simply scratched off the Nippon mark. Some marks were even removed with the aid of scouring powder or acid. Items sold in Japan did not have to be marked and employees of American based companies in Japan, visitors and missionaries might have brought some of these items back with their household goods when they returned to the United States. Other countries where Nippon was exported may have been less strigent than the United States and did not require the country of origin to be stamped on the imported wares. These items may have later been brought to our shores. Some unmarked articles may merely have been manufactured before the 1891 law, others after 1921 with a paper label affixed which has subsequently been removed.

How does one know when an item is Nippon although it is not marked as such? First, you must get the 'feel' of Nippon; observe and handle many marked specimens. Touch them. See how these pieces vary from others. George Palmer once wrote "The first rule shall be observe! A simple matter, one, I dare say, which it will seem to you difficult not to follow. You have a pair of eyes; how can you fail to observe? Ah? but eyes can only look; that is not observing. You want to observe, not to look only. It makes all the difference whether you do thus observe, whether you are willing to hold your attention to the thing in hand and see what it contains."

If the work is definitely characteristic of Oriental craftsmen, the item appears to be old, I like it and if it is in good condition and the price is right I would purchase it. A well made item is still worth collecting whether it is marked or not. A collector should buy because the item appeals to him for its beauty and decoration.

However, do let me add that some blanks of china are being imported today in our country from Japan bearing paper labels on the bottom. These can be easily removed. The items are then handpainted and some are being peddled to unsuspecting persons as authentic unmarked Nippon. Copyists and fake items are always with us especially now that Nippon items are commanding higher prices. Years ago it would not have been very profitable to counterfeit these items as their price was so low.

In Dorothy Hammond's book *"Confusing Collectibles"*, she has an article about fake marks which I found very interesting. It was listed under R.S. Prussia items and stated that new stickers were being made and placed on articles which were not marked. The actual pieces were not faked or duplicated, they were merely unmarked items getting new marks fired on them. She was even able to locate a West Coast dealer who actually sent her a sheet of the R.S. Prussia decals along with firing instructions. She states that the mark was "skillfully produced, it would fool any collector or dealer". We not only have to worry about fake items but also fake marks! As the old saying goes, when in doubt, go without. If you are at all suspicious about a mark or item, simply refuse to buy the article.

The collecting and classification of marks on Nippon porcelain can be both fun and fascinating but it should not obscure one's interest. Actually, we should be more impressed with the artistic work, the style, the workmanship and the beauty of the item. Perhaps it should just be a matter of locating these different marks that should give us pleasure.

The acquisition of Nippon porcelain can be exciting and educational as well as one of lasting value. The purchase of one piece usually leads to another and another until the china cabinets and cupboards start overflowing. It is almost as though they were magnets attracting each other. "Nipponaholics" just can't seem to stop their addiction. There seems to be no known cure but then most of us are not even searching for one.

The collector is an incurable romantic. Collecting gives us a glimpse of the past, hope of discovering 'the find' in the future while still giving us beauty and joy from day to day. These beautiful items were not made by chance! Sir Joshua Reynolds once wrote "Excellence is never granted to man but as the reward of labor." Care for your dishes and live with them! The more you use them, the more you get to enjoy their beauty.

Hand drawn facsimiles of marks found on Nippon items

BABY BUD NIPPON

1. Baby Bud Nippon
   incised on doll

2. Bara hand painted Nippon

3. Carpathia M Nippon

4. Cherry blossom hand painted Nippon
   found in blue, green & magenta colors

5. Cherry blossom in a circle
   hand painted Nippon

6. Chikusa hand painted Nippon

7. China E-OH hand painted
   Nippon found in blue & green colors

8. Crown (pointed), hand painted Nippon
   found in green & blue colors

9. Crown Nippon (pointed), Made in Nippon
   found in green and blue colors

10. Crown (square), hand painted Nippon
    found in green and green with red colors

11. Chubby LW & Co. Nippon
found on dolls

15. Double T Diamond in circle Nippon

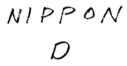

12. D Nippon

16. Dowsie Nippon

13. Dolly sticker found on Nippon's Dolly dolls,
sold by Morimure Bros.

17. EE Nippon

14. Double T Diamond, Nippon

18. Elite B hand painted Nippon

NIPPON
401

19. FY 401 Nippon
found on dolls

23. Hand painted Nippon

FY
NIPPON
405

20. FY 405 Nippon
found on dolls

24. Hand painted Nippon

HAND PAINTED
NIPPON

25. Hand painted Nippon

Hand Painted
G
NIPPON

21. G in a circle
hand painted Nippon

Hand Painted
NIPPON

26. Hand painted Nippon

Hand painted
GLORIA
L. W. & C₀.
NIPPON

22. Gloria L.W. & Co. hand painted Nippon
(Louis Wolf Co., Boston, Mass. & N.Y.C.)

Handpainted
NIPPON

27. Hand painted Nippon

28. Hand painted Nippon with symbol

33. Hand painted Nippon with symbol

29. Hand painted Nippon with symbol

34. Hand painted Nippon with symbol

30. Hand painted Nippon with symbol

31. Hand painted Nippon with symbol

35. Hand painted Nippon with symbol

32. Hand painted Nippon with symbol

36. Horsman No. 1 Nippon
found on dolls

37. IC Nippon

38. Imperial Nippon
found in blue & green

39. JMDS Nippon

40. Jonroth Studio hand painted Nippon

41. Kid Doll M.W. & Co. Nippon

42. Kinjo Nippon

43. Kinjo China hand painted Nippon

44. L & Co. Nippon

45. LFH hand painted Nippon

46. LW & Co. Nippon (Louis Wolf & Co.,
Boston, Mass & N.Y.C.)

47. M in wreath, hand painted Nippon
(M stands for importer, Morimura Bros.)
found in green, blue, magenta & gold colors

48. M in wreath hand painted Nippon, D.M. Read Co.
(M stands for importer, Morimura Bros.)

49. M B (Morimura Bros.)
Baby Darling sticker
found on dolls

50. M M hand painted Nippon

MADE IN
NIPPON

51. Made in Nippon

52. Maple leaf Nippon
found in green, blue & magenta

53. Morimura Bros.
sticker found on Nippon items

54. Mt. Fujiyama Nippon

NIPPON

55. Nippon
found in blue, gold and also incised into items

NIPPON 84

56. Nippon 84

NIPPON 144

57. Nippon 144

221
NIPPON

58. Nippon 221

59. Nippon with symbol

60. Nippon with symbol

NIPPON

61. Nippon with symbol

NIPPON

62. Nippon with symbol

63. Nippon with symbol

502
NO. 70018
NIPPON

64. Nippon with symbol

65. Nippon M incised on doll
(note N is written backwards)
#12 denotes size of doll
M = Morimura Bros.

66. Noritake M in wreath Nippon
    M = Morimura Bros.
    found in green, blue & magenta

67. Noritake Nippon
    found in green, blue & magenta colors

68. Noritake Nippon
    found in green, blue & magenta colors

69. OAC Hand painted Nippon
    (Okura Art China, branch of Noritake Co.)

70. Oriental china Nippon

71. Pagoda hand painted Nippon

PATENT
NO 30441
NIPPON

72. Patent #30441 Nippon

73. Paulownia flowers & leaves
    hand painted Nippon (crest used
    by Empress of Japan, kiri no mon)
    found in a green/red color

74. Paulownia flowers & leaves
    hand painted Nippon (crest used by
    Empress of Japan, kiri no mon)

39

75. Pickard etched china, Noritake Nippon
Pickard mark is in black
Noritake/Nippon mark is blue in color

79. RC Nippon

76. Pickard hand painted china Nippon

80. RC hand painted Nippon
combination of both red & green colors

81. RC Noritake Nippon hand painted
found in green & blue

77. Pickard hand-painted china, Noritake Nippon
Pickard mark printed in black
Noritake Nippon in magenta

82. RC Noritake Nippon

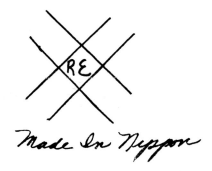

83. RE Nippon

84. Rising Sun Nippon

85. Royal Dragon Nippon

86. Royal Dragon Nippon
Studio hand painted

87. Royal Kaga Nippon

88. Royal Kinran Nippon
found in blue, gold colors

89. Royal Kinran Crown Nippon
found in blue, gold & green colors

90. Royal Moriye Nippon
found in green & blue colors

91. Royal Nishiki Nippon

92. Royal Satsuma Nippon
(cross within a ring, crest of Prince of Satsuma)

93. Royal Sometuke Nippon

94. Royal Sometuke Nippon Sicily

95. R.S Nippon

96. S & K hand painted Nippon
found in green, blue & magenta colors

97. S & K hand painted Nippon
found in green, blue & magenta colors

98. Shinzo Nippon

99. Shofu Nagoya Nippon

100. SNB Nippon

104. Studio hand painted Nippon

101. SNB Nagoya Nippon

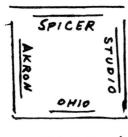

102. Spicer Studio Akron Ohio Nippon
    *(See Page 45)

105. Superior hand painted Nippon

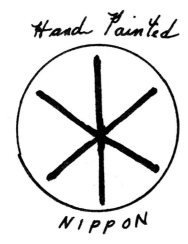

103. Spoke hand painted Nippon

106. T Nippon
    (2 hō-ō birds)

107. T hand painted Nippon

111. TS hand painted Nippon

108. T in wreath hand painted Nippon

112. Teacup Nippon

109. T N hand painted Nippon
     mark is red & green

113. Torii Nippon

110. TS hand painted Nippon

114. Tree crest Nippon
     (crest of Morimura family)

44

117. Yamato hand painted Nippon

115. Tree Crest & Maple leaf hand painted Nippon

118. Yamato Nippon

116. V Nippon, Scranton, Pa.

* According to Jabe Tarter who writes a column on antiques for the Knight-Ridder Newspaper chain, the Spicer Studios were located on Spicer St. in the old Spicer home. The street and village were named for Judge William Spicer and in the years of 1885 to 1915 there were schools of decorating in the area, at the time called Spicer Town. Each class was required to put the name Spicer Studio on their wares but most of the time they were also permitted to place their own name on as the artist as well. The one which was called Spicer rather than Spicer Town as the others were is the best of them all. The paintings on china and porcelain coming from there are avidly sought by collectors of the Akron area. Spicer Town Studios was the owner of the compound. The Spicer Studio was in operation from 1885 to 1910. Mrs. Eva Gifford was the head instructor of the hand painting classes.

Plate 1

Cobalt and gold overlay vase, 7½" high, blue mark #52

Plate 2

Cobalt and scenic vase, 8½" tall, green mark #47

Plate 3

Cobalt and scenic vase, 8" tall, green mark #47

Plate 4

Cobalt and scenic teapot, 6" tall, green mark #47

Plate 5

Cobalt and scenic vase, 8¾" tall, blue mark #52

Plate 6

Cobalt and scenic vase, 9" tall, blue mark #52

Plate 1

Plate 2

Plate 3

Plate 4

Plate 5

Plate 6

47

Plate 7

Cobalt and floral vase (also has heavy gold overlay), 7½" tall, blue mark #47
Cobalt and gold overlay vase, 7" tall, blue mark #52
Cobalt and floral ewer, 10" tall, blue mark #89

Plate 8

Cobalt, gold and floral chocolate pot and cups and saucers, pot is 10" tall, all pieces are marked with blue mark #52

Plate 7

Plate 8

49

Plate 9

Cobalt vase with heavy silver overlay, 6½" tall, green mark #79
Cobalt vase with heavy gold overlay, 10" tall, blue mark #52

Plate 10

Top Row:
Vase, 6½" tall, cobalt and floral, blue mark #52
Bottom Row:
Cobalt and floral calling card tray, 7½" long, blue mark #52
Ewer, 11" tall, cobalt and floral, green mark #52

Plate 11

Cobalt and floral covered urn, 13" tall, blue mark #52

Plate 12

Cobalt and gold basket vase, 7¾" tall, green mark #47
Vase, 7¼" tall, cobalt, gold and floral decoration, blue mark #52

Plate 9

Plate 11

Plate 10

Plate 12

51

Plate 13

Cobalt and gold chocolate set consisting of 10" high chocolate pot, 11¾" wide tray and matching creamer and sugar, blue mark #47

Plate 14

Four matching cobalt and gold bouillon cups with underplates, each 4¼" high, green mark #47

Matching cobalt and gold cup and saucer, unmarked

Plate 13

Plate 14

53

Plate 15

Cobalt and floral cake set. Large cake platter is 10½" wide and the matching cake plates are 6¼" wide. All have blue mark #52

Plate 16

Cobalt and floral cookie jar, 7¾" in height, blue mark #52

Matching plate, 8¾" in diameter, blue mark #52

Plate 15

Plate 16

Plate 17

Matching scenic cobalt plates each 8½" in diameter, both having the green mark #47

Plate 18

Cobalt scenic plate, 10" in diameter, green mark #47
Matching scene on cobalt cake platter, 10¾" in diameter, green mark #47

Plate 19

Cobalt and gold plate, 10" in diameter, green mark #47
Cobalt scenic tray, 11¼" long having the blue mark #52

Plate 17

Plate 18

Plate 19

Plate 20

Tapestry vase, scenic decor, 6¼" tall, blue mark #52

Plate 21

Tapestry vase, 6" tall, blue mark #52
Tapestry vase, 7¼" tall, blue mark #52

Plate 22

Tapestry vase, 9½" tall, blue mark #52

Plate 23

Tapestry vase with moriage decorated owl, 12¼" tall, green mark #91

Plate 24

Tapestry humidor with moriage decorated owl, 6½" tall, green mark #52
Tapestry humidor with scenic decor, 6½" tall, blue mark #52

Plate 25

Tapestry vase, 6" tall, blue mark #52

Plate 26

Tapestry vase, 6" tall, green mark #52
Tapestry vase, 9" tall, green mark #52
Tapestry vase, 6" tall, green mark #52

Plate 20

Plate 21

Plate 22

Plate 23

Plate 24

Plate 25

Plate 26

59

Plate 27

Wedgwood vase, 8" tall, green mark #47

Plate 28

Wedgwood decorated tray, 11" long, green mark #10
Matching wedgwood ashtray, 2½" in diameter, green mark #10

Plate 29

Wedgwood compote, 5¼" tall, green mark #47
Wedgwood humidor, diamond shaped, 4½" tall, green mark #47
Wedgwood vase, 7¼" tall, green mark #47

Plate 30

Wedgwood decorated bowl, 7¼" wide including handles, green mark #47

Plate 31

Wedgwood and floral decorated creamer and sugar set, sugar bowl is 5" tall,
creamer is 3" tall, green mark #47

Plate 27

Plate 28

Plate 29

Plate 30

Plate 31

61

Plate 32

Vase with portrait of Countess Anna Potocka, 7½" tall, green mark #52
Vase, 7½" tall, blue mark #52

Plate 33

Powder box, 5¼" wide, blue mark #52
Powder box, 4½" wide, blue mark #52
Hair receiver, 4½" wide, blue mark #52

Plate 34

Covered urn, 14" tall, blue mark #52

Plate 35

Vase, 12¼" tall, green mark #52 (portrait of Countess Anna Potocka)

Plate 36

Top Row:
Vase, 6¾" tall, green mark #52
Vase, 8½" tall, blue mark #52
Bottom Row:
Vase, 5½" tall, blue mark #52
Sugar bowl, 6" tall, blue mark #52

Plate 32

Plate 34

Plate 33

Plate 35

Plate 36

63

Plate 37

All items have gold background with pink roses, each is covered with tourquoise colored dots of enameling.

Top Row:

7" vase, blue mark #52

Creamer and sugar set, 4½" tall, green mark #52

Vase, 5" high, green mark #52

Bottom Row:

Vase 9¼" high, green mark #52

Sugar and creamer set, sugar bowl is 2¾" high, green mark #52

Pitcher, 4" high, blue mark #70

Vase 3¼" tall, unmarked

Vase 8¾" high, blue mark #89

Plate 38

Gold beaded and scenic items, footed bowl, 7¼" in diameter, blue mark #52

Powder box 5¾" in diameter, blue mark #52

Covered urn, 9¼" tall, unmarked

Plate 37

Plate 38

Plate 39

Large covered urn (artist signed), 19" high, green mark #47

Plate 40

Covered urn, 15¼" tall, green mark #47

Plate 41

Urn, 13¾" tall, green mark #47

Plate 42

Urn, 10½" tall, blue mark #52

Plate 39

Plate 40

Plate 41

Plate 42

Plate 43

Ewer, 9¾" high, blue mark #52

Plate 44

Ferner, 5¾" high, 10½" wide including handles, green mark #47

Plate 45

Vase, 8½" tall, unmarked

Plate 46

Vase, 10¼" tall, green mark #52

Plate 47

Cookie jar, 7½" tall, blue mark #52

Plate 48

Vase, 9½" tall, green mark #52

Plate 43

Plate 44

Plate 45

Plate 46

Plate 47

Plate 48

Plate 49

Top Row:
    Vase, 7" tall, blue mark #52
    Basket vase, 7" tall, unmarked
Second Row:
    Vase, 7¾" high, blue mark #52
Bottom Row:
    Vase, 10" tall, blue mark #52
    Vase, 9" tall, blue mark #52

Plate 50

    Vase, 9¼" tall, green mark #52

Plate 51

    Humidor, 5½" tall, blue mark #52
    Humidor, 5½" tall, blue mark #52

Plate 52

    Candlestick lamp, 13" tall, blue mark #52

Plate 50

Plate 49

Plate 51

Plate 52

Plate 53

Vase, 13¾" high, blue mark #52

Plate 54

Bowl, 10¾" in diameter, green mark #52; bowl, 12" in diameter, green mark #52

Plate 55

Vase, 9" tall, blue mark #52; bowl, 11" in diameter, blue mark #52

Plate 56

Vase, 12" tall, blue mark #52

Plate 57

Cookie jar with underplate, 8" tall, green mark #81

Plate 53

Plate 54

Plate 55

Plate 56

Plate 57

Plate 58

Chocolate pot and four matching cups and saucers, pot measures 11½" in height, mark has been scratched off

Plate 59

Chocolate pot, five matching cups and saucers and matching footed bowl. Pot measures 9¾" tall and bowl is 7½" in diameter. All pieces have the blue mark #52

Plate 58

Plate 59

75

Plate 60

Cookie jar, 8" tall, blue mark #52
Cake plate, 11¼" wide, blue mark #52

Plate 61

Bowl, 11" in diameter, green mark #52

Plate 62

Bowl, 12" in diameter, blue mark #52

Plate 63

Bowl, 11" in diameter, green mark #52

Plate 64

Chocolate pot, 10" tall, blue mark #52
Chocolate pot, 9¾" tall, green mark #47
Chocolate pot, 9¾" tall, blue mark #52

Plate 60

Plate 61

Plate 62

Plate 63

Plate 64

Plate 65

Dresser set composed of 11¼" long tray, hair receiver, hatpin holder which is 4¾" tall, trinket box and powder box, all are marked with blue mark #52

Plate 66

Matching plate and dresser set. Plate measures 8½" in diameter, three piece dresser set consists of 11" long tray and powder box and hair receiver, all are marked with green mark #52

Plate 65

Plate 66

Plate 67

Berry set, large bowl is 9¾" in diameter, small bowls are 5¼" in diameter, all have green mark #47

Plate 68

Matching tea set, teapot is 6½" tall, all marked with green mark #47, set comes with four cups and saucers, teapot, creamer and sugar bowl.

Plate 67

Plate 68

Plate 69

Cake plate, 11½" in diameter, blue mark #52
Syrup with underplate, 6" in height, green mark #50

Plate 70

Ferner, 10½" in diameter including handles, 5¾" high, green mark #47

Plate 71

Ferner, 10½" in diameter including handles, 5¾" high, green mark #47

Plate 72

Plate, 7½" in diameter, green mark #81
Cake plate, 10½" in diameter, blue mark #47
Plate, 7½" in diameter, blue mark #52

Plate 73

Ferner, 7¾" in diameter, 4¼" high, green mark #47

Plate 74

Bowl, 7½" in diameter, blue mark #52
Bowl, 4¾" in diameter, blue mark #52
Bowl, 7½" in diameter, blue mark #52

Plate 69

Plate 70

Plate 71

Plate 72

Plate 73

Plate 74

Plate 75

Bowl, 7¾" wide, mark #80
Bowl, 8¾" wide, blue mark #47

Plate 76

Three handled nappy, 6¼" wide, blue mark #52
Bowl, 5¾" wide, blue mark #52

Plate 77

Sauce dish and underplate, underplate is 7" long, sauce is 2½" tall, blue mark #52
Matching cake plate, 6¼" wide, green mark #52
Sauce dish with matching underplate, underplate is 7" long, sauce is 2¼" tall, blue mark #52

Plate 78

Cake set, cake platter is 10½" wide, six cake plates are 6¼" wide, all are marked with green mark #47

Plate 79

Berry bowl with underplate, underplate is 8¾" wide, blue mark #52
Berry bowl with underplate, underplate is 8¼" wide, blue mark #52

Plate 75

Plate 76

Plate 77

Plate 78

Plate 79

Plate 80

Top Row:

Cookie jar, 8½" tall, blue mark #52

Bowl, 8½" in diameter, mark #80

Bottom Row:

Tea set, teapot is 5½" tall, sugar bowl, creamer and four footed cups, all have blue mark #52

Plate 81

Top Row:

Bowl, 9¾" in diameter, green mark #52

Pair of matching cups and saucers, blue mark #52

Bottom Row:

Tea set consisting of teapot which is 5¼" tall and sugar bowl and creamer, have blue mark #47

Candy dish, 7" wide including handle, blue mark #52

Plate 80

Plate 81

Plate 82

Luncheon set consisting of a total of 72 pieces

Top Row:

Large 9¾" bowl, blue mark #47

Chocolate pot, 8¼" tall, blue mark #47

Cake platter which is 10¾" wide, blue mark #47

Middle Row:

Candy dish, 6½" wide, blue mark #47

Cup and saucer, blue mark #47

Three sizes of plates, 6¼", 7½", and 8½", all green mark #47

Two piece tea strainer, 1¾" tall, green mark #47

Compote, 2½" high, blue mark #47

Sauce dish and ladle, 5½" in diameter, blue mark #47

Bottom Row:

Celery dish, 13¼" in length, blue mark #47

Individual salt, 3¾" long, blue mark #47

Nut cup, 3" in width, green mark #47

Mustard jar and spoon with attached underplate which is 4½" in diameter, blue mark #47

Plate 82

89

Plate 83

Top Row:
> Moriage decorated vase, 9" tall, blue mark #52
> Moriage ewer, 7½" tall, blue mark #47
> Moriage vase, has three handles, 5¾" tall, blue mark #47

Bottom Row:
> Moriage candlestick, triangular shaped, 8¼" tall, blue mark #47
> Moriage hanging placque, 10" diameter, blue mark #47
> Moriage vase, 10" tall, blue mark #47

Plate 84

Moriage decorated chocolate set. Pot is 10½" tall, set has four cups and saucers, blue mark #71

Plate 83

Plate 84

Plate 85

Moriage vase, 9" tall, blue mark #52

Plate 86

Moriage decorated bowl, 10" in diameter, blue mark #52

Plate 87

Moriage vase, 6½" tall, green mark #52
Moriage pitcher, 7½" tall, blue mark #16

Plate 88

Moriage bowl, 9" in diameter, blue mark #52

Plate 89

Moriage ewer, 8½" tall, blue mark #52
Moriage vase, 8" tall, green mark #52

Plate 90

Moriage decorated vase, 10" tall, blue mark #115

Plate 85

Plate 86

Plate 87

Plate 88

Plate 89

Plate 90

93

Plate 91

Moriage decorated bowl, 9¾" diameter, blue mark #52
Moriage decorated footed bowl, 9¼" long, green mark #90

Plate 92

Moriage decorated vase, 4½" tall, blue mark #52

Plate 93

Moriage vase, 5" tall, green mark #47
Moriage footed bowl, 8½" long, blue mark #90
Moriage rose bowl, 5¾" wide, blue mark #52

Plate 94

Moriage decorated humidor, 5½" tall, green mark #47

Plate 95

Moriage humidor, 7" tall, blue mark #52
Moriage humidor, 6" tall, blue mark #52

Plate 96

Moriage vase, 5½" tall, green mark #52

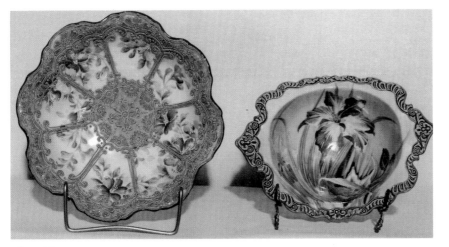

Plate 91

Plate 92

Plate 93

Plate 94

Plate 95

Plate 96

Plate 97

Moriage decorated ferner, 7½" in diameter, blue mark #52
Moriage cookie jar, 7" tall, green mark #47

Plate 98

Moriage vase, 7½" tall, blue mark #47
Moriage vase, 8¼" tall, blue mark #47

Plate 99

Moriage decorated ewer, 7½" tall, blue mark #16
Moriage decorated compote, 4¼" in diameter, unmarked
Moriage handled candlestick, 6¾" tall, unmarked

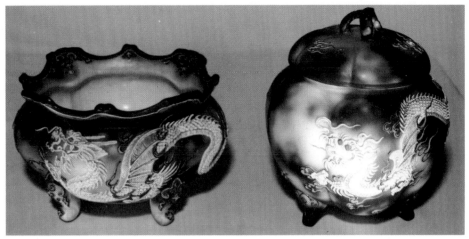

Plate 97

Plate 98

Plate 99

Plate 100

Relief molded tankard set consists of 11½" tall tankard and four mugs which are 5" in height, all have green mark #47

Plate 101

Relief molded humidor, 7½" tall. Has a scene depicting 12 monks and priests, 3 animals, ram, dragon and foo dog. Humidor is marked with the blue mark #52

Humidor, 7½" in height, green mark #47, has a Grecian scene depicting 14 women, top is adorned with grapes and leaves.

Plate 100

Plate 101

All items molded in relief

Plate 102

Vase, 9½" tall, green mark #52
Vase, 8½" tall, blue mark #52

Plate 103

Vase, 9¾" tall, green mark #52

Plate 104

Vase, 6½" tall, green mark #47

Plate 105

Handled basket dish, 7½" wide, 6" high, green mark #47

Plate 106

Vase, 8¼" tall, green mark #47

Plate 107

Vase, 10" tall, green mark #47

Plate 102

Plate 103

Plate 104

Plate 105

Plate 106

Plate 107

All items molded in relief

Plate 108

Humidor, 6½" tall, hieroglyphics are incised into body of item, figures are those of Egyptian Goddess, a Pharoh and a Sphinx, green mark #47

Plate 109

Humidor, 6" tall, green mark #47
Humidor, 6" tall, green mark #47
Humidor, 6" tall, green mark #47

Plate 110

Ashtray, 7" long, green mark #47
Ashtray, 5" in diameter, green mark #47
Ashtray, 7" long, green mark #47

Plate 111

Humidor, 6" high, green mark #47

Plate 112

Humidor, 7½" tall, green mark #47
Humidor, 7" tall, green mark #47

Plate 113

Stein, 7" tall, displays different dogs, leash is twisted around handle, green mark #47

Plate 108

Plate 109

Plate 110

Plate 111

Plate 112

Plate 113

All items molded in relief

Plate 114

Bowl with molded peanuts, 7" in diameter, green mark #47

Plate 115

Bowl with molded acorns, 7¾" in diameter, green mark #47

Plate 116

Bowl with molded chestnuts, 7¾" in diameter, green mark #47

Plate 117

Hanging placque, 10½" in diameter, green mark #47

Plate 118

Hanging placque, 10½" in diameter, green mark #47

Plate 119

Hanging placque, 10½" in diameter, green mark #47

Plate 120

Hanging placque, 10½" in diameter, green mark #47

Plate 114

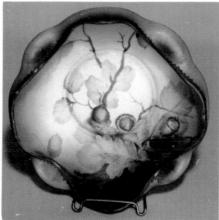

Plate 115

Plate 116

Plate 117

Plate 118

Plate 119

Plate 120

All items molded in relief

Plate 121

Hanging placque, 10½" in diameter, green mark #47
Hanging placque, 10½" in diameter, green mark #47
Hanging placque, 10½" in diameter, green mark #47

Plate 122

Hanging placque, 10½" in diameter, green mark #47
Hanging placque, 10½" in diameter, green mark #47
Hanging placque, 10½" in diameter, green mark #47

Plate 123

Hanging placque, 10½" in diameter, green mark #47
Hanging placque, 10½" in diameter, green mark #47
Hanging placque, 10½" in diameter, green mark #47

Plate 121

Plate 122

Plate 123

107

All pieces decorated with American Indian decor

Plate 124

Top Row:
Hanging placque, 8" diameter, green mark #47
Middle Row:
Relish dish, 8½" long, green mark #47
Bottom Row:
Relish dish, 8½" long, green mark #47

Plate 125

Hanging placque, 10½" in diameter, blue mark #52

Plate 126

Bowl, 8" in diameter including handles, green mark #47

Plate 127

Molded in relief ashtray and match holder, 6½" wide, green mark #47

Plate 128

Humidor, 6" tall, green mark #47
Humidor, 5¾" tall, green mark #47
Humidor, 6" tall, green mark #47

Plate 129

Relief molded humidor, 6" tall, green mark #47

Plate 125

Plate 124

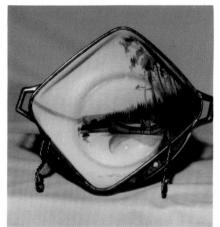

Plate 127

Plate 126

Plate 129

Plate 128

All souvenir or advertising items

Plate 130

All items have a picture of the Capitol Building in Washington D.C.
Top Row:
    Tray, 8¾" long, blue mark #52
    Pin box, 2" in diameter, 1¼" high, green mark #47
    Basket dish, 6½" long, blue mark #52
    Individual salt, 2½" long, green mark #47
    Demitasse pot, 6¾" high, blue mark #52
Bottom Row:
    Handled nappy, 5½" wide, red mark #47
    Sugar and creamer matching above demitasse pot, blue mark #52
    Individual salt, 3¾" long, green mark #47

Plate 131

Top Row:
    Vase inscribed Toronto Exhibition 1919, 5¼" tall, green mark #86
    Ink blotter having gold sticker #53, 4¼" long, also has red mark #47
Bottom Row:
    Powder box with inscription Newport, R.I., 3" high, green mark #47
    Small dish, souvenir of Portland, Me., 5" long, blue mark #84
    Handled nappy, 6¼" wide, blue mark #48, souvenir of Fair Week 1912

Plate 130

Plate 131

Plate 132

Child's tea set, consists of teapot which is 3½" tall, creamer and sugar bowl and 4 cups, saucers and plates, blue mark #84
Boy doll, 16½" tall, incised with mark #65

Plate 133

Doll, 4¾" tall, incised with mark #55
Doll, 4" tall, incised with mark #55
Child's tea set consisting of child's face teapot which is 3½" tall, and four cups 1¼" tall, blue mark #55

Plate 132

Plate 133

113

Plate 134

Top Row:

Doll, 7" tall, incised with mark #46

Bride and groom, 5" tall, bride only incised with mark #55

Baby Bud doll, 5" tall, incised with mark #1

Doll, 4¾" tall, incised with mark #56

Doll, 6¼" tall, incised with mark 55

Bottom Row:

Child's tea set consisting of teapot, creamer, sugar bowl, six cups, saucers and plates, blue mark #71

Doll, 9" tall, incised with mark #55

Plate 135

Top Row:

Happifats, 3½" tall, incised with mark #55

Doll, 3½" tall, incised with mark #55

Doll, 4½" tall, incised with mark #55

Doll, 5" tall, incised with mark #57

Bottom Row:

Dutch boy, 3¾" tall, incised with mark #55

Doll, 3¾" tall, incised with mark #55

Baby Bud, 3¾" tall, incised with mark #55

Medic uniformed doll, has red cross on case, 3¾" tall, incised with mark #55

Policeman with club in his hand, 3¾" tall, incised with mark #55

Plate 134

Plate 135

115

Plate 136

Doll, 7" tall, incised with mark #46
Two small plates, 5" in diameter, green mark #81
Doll in rocking chair, 7¼" tall, incised with mark #55
Child's play tea set, teapot is 4" tall, blue mark #84

Plate 137

Child's feeding dish, 8" in diameter, blue mark #84
Doll, 5" tall, incised with mark #55
Baby Darling doll, 4¾" tall, mark #49
Baby mug, 2½" tall, blue mark #84
Child's mug, 3" tall, blue mark #84

Plate 136

Plate 137

117

Plate 138

Child's play tea set, consists of teapot which is 4" tall, creamer and sugar bowl and four cups, saucers and plates. All are marked with blue mark #84
Doll, 24" tall, composition body, incised mark #20

Plate 139

Top Row:

      Doll, 5¼" tall, incised with mark #55

      Child's bowl, 5¾" in diameter, blue mark #84

      Hanging plate, 6" in diameter, blue mark #84

      Pincushion doll, 5" tall, incised with mark #55

Bottom Row:

      Boy doll, 9¼" tall, incised with mark #55

      Child's creamer, 3¼" tall, blue mark #84

      Child's cup, 2½" tall, blue mark #84

      Doll with grass skirt, 5" tall, incised with mark #55

      Child's plate, 6¾" in diameter, blue mark #84

Plate 138

Plate 139

Plate 140

Pickard decorated gold etched vase, artist signed by A. Richter, 6" tall, mark #75

Pickard decorated gold etched bowl, 7" wide, mark #77

Plate 141

Vase with heavily applied enamel glaze resembling pottery, 8" tall, green mark #47

Matching potpourri jar, 6½" tall, green mark #47

Matching stick vase, 10½" tall, green mark #47

Plate 142

Bowl imitating Gouda ceramics, 9¼" in diameter, green mark #47

Matching candlestick, 8" in height, green mark #47

Plate 143

Vase, 9¼" tall, has heavy gold overlay, green mark #74

Plate 144

Vase, 3½" tall, leaves are done in heavy gold overlay, blue mark #52

Matching vase, 7½" tall, blue mark #52

Plate 145

Vase, 4" tall, cloisonné on porcelain, gold mark #55

Plate 141

Plate 140

Plate 142

Plate 143

Plate 144

Plate 145

121

Plate 146

Mantle set consisting of pair of candlesticks, 8" tall and vase, 8" tall. All pieces are cloisonné on porcelain and all have green mark #47

Plate 147

Stein, 7" tall, cloisonné on porcelain, green mark #47

Plate 148

Bowl, artist signed Kimu, 12½" long, green mark #47

Plate 149

Vase, 12" tall, has applied work that has been incised, blue mark #38

Plate 150

Compote, 3½" tall, top is 7¾" in diameter, base is triangular in shape with three sphinx figures supporting dish, green mark #47

Plate 151

Humidor, 4" tall with sprigged-on pipe, green mark #47

Plate 152

Vase, 7" tall, has coralene beading, reddish brown mark #95

Plate 146

Plate 147

Plate 148

Plate 149

Plate 150

Plate 151

Plate 152

123

Plate 153

All items are in Azalea pattern, all are marked with blue mark #84. Cup and saucer are slightly larger than those found with Noritake backstamp.
Sugar bowl is 3 5/8" tall, creamer is 3 1/8" tall
Plates are 6½" in diameter and 7¾" in diameter
Mayonnaise with ladle, bowl is 4½" in diameter

Plate 154

Ashtray, 5½" wide, green mark #47

Plate 155

All four items display old fashioned airplanes, those manufactured around World War I. Hatpin holder is 4½" tall, has green mark #47
Shaving mug is 3½" tall, green mark #47
Ashtray, 5½" wide, green mark #47
Hanging double matchbox holder, 5" long, green mark #47

Plate 156

Novelty item, comic face of Jiggs, green mark #47
Figural ashtray, blue mark #47

Plate 153

Plate 154

Plate 155

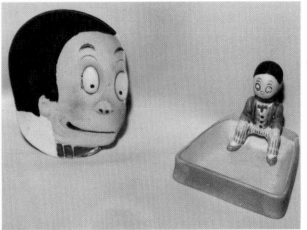

Plate 156

Plate 157

Top Row:

Wine jug, English coach scene, 9½" high, blue mark #52

Wine jug, portrait of monk, 9½" high, green mark #47

Wine jug, scene of birds, one done in moriage decoration, 9½" high, blue mark #52

Middle Row:

Wine jug, 8¼" high, scene of stag in the forest, blue mark #47

Wine jug with scene of Russian dancers, 9½" high, green mark #47

Bottom Row:

Wine jug with desert scene, 9½" high, green mark #47

Wine jug with scene of lady and two children, 9½" high, green mark #47

Plate 157

127

Plate 158

Stein, 7" tall, green mark #47
Stein, 7" tall, green mark #47

Plate 159

Whiskey jug, 7" tall, blue mark #52
Whiskey jug, 6" tall, blue mark #52

Plate 160

Stein, 7" tall, woodland scene, blue mark #52
Matching whiskey jug, 7" tall, blue mark #52

Plate 161

Wine jug, 11" tall, blue mark #52
Wine jug, 11" tall, blue mark #52

Plate 158

Plate 159

Plate 160

Plate 161

129

Plate 162

Whiskey jug, 5½" tall, green mark #47
Whiskey jug, 7" tall, signed with name of dog, Champion L'Ambassadeur, green mark #47

Plate 163

Whiskey jug, 8" tall, green mark #47
Whiskey jug, 7" tall, green mark #47

Plate 164

Whiskey jug, 7½" tall, blue mark #47
Whiskey jug, 7½" tall, blue mark #52

Plate 165

Tankard, 13¾" tall, blue mark #52

Plate 166

Mug, 4¾" tall, green mark #52

Plate 162

Plate 163

Plate 165

Plate 164

Plate 166

131

Plate 167

Stein, 7" high, green mark #47
Stein, 7" high, blue mark #52
Stein, 7" high, blue mark #52

Plate 168

Wine jug, 7¾" high, blue mark #52
Wine jug, 10" high, blue mark #52
Wine jug, 7¾" high, blue mark #52

Plate 169

Stein, 7" high, green mark #47
Stein, 7" high, green mark #47
Stein, 7" high, green mark #47

Plate 167

Plate 168

Plate 169

Plate 170

    Humidor, 5" tall, green mark #47
    Humidor, 5½" tall, green mark #47
    Humidor, 4½" tall, green mark #47

Plate 171

    Humidor, 6" tall, green mark #47
    Humidor, 6" tall, green mark #47
    Humidor, 6" tall, green mark #47

Plate 172

    Humidor, 5½" tall, green mark #47
    Humidor, 4" tall, green mark #47
    Humidor, 5" tall, green mark #47

Plate 173

    Humidor, 6½" tall, green mark #47
    Humidor, 4" tall, green mark #47
    Humidor, 5½" tall, green mark #47

Plate 170

Plate 171

Plate 172

Plate 173

Plate 174

Humidor, 7½" tall, green mark #47
Humidor, 7½" tall, green mark #47

Plate 175

Humidor, 7" tall, green mark #47
Humidor, 7½" tall, green mark #47

Plate 176

Humidor, 5½" tall, green mark #47
Humidor, 9¾" tall, blue mark #47
Humidor, 6½" tall, green mark #47

Plate 177

Humidor, 7" tall, green mark #47

Plate 178

Humidor, 6½" tall, blue mark #52
Humidor, 8¼" tall, blue mark #52
Humidor, 6½" tall, green mark #47

Plate 179

Humidor, 6½" tall, green mark #47

Plate 174

Plate 175

Plate 176

Plate 177

Plate 178

Plate 179

Plate 180

    Humidor, 5½" tall, blue mark #52
    Humidor, 5½" tall, green mark #47

Plate 181

    Humidor, 7½" tall, green mark #47
    Humidor, 7½" tall, green mark #47

Plate 182

    Humidor, 6" tall, green mark #47
    Humidor, 6" tall, green mark #47

Plate 183

    Humidor, 6½" tall, green mark #47
    Humidor, 6" tall, green mark #47

Plate 184

    Humidor, 6½" tall, blue mark #52
    Humidor, 6½" tall, blue mark #52

Plate 185

    Humidor, 7½" tall, green mark #47
    Humidor, 7½" tall, green mark #47

Plate 180

Plate 181

Plate 182

Plate 183

Plate 184

Plate 185

Plate 186

Humidor, 5½" tall, green mark #47
Humidor, 5½" tall, green mark #47

Plate 187

Humidor, 7" tall, blue mark #52
Humidor, 5½" tall, green mark #47

Plate 188

Humidor, 6" tall, blue mark #52
Humidor, 5" tall, green mark #47

Plate 189

Humidor, 7" tall, green mark #47

Plate 190

Humidor, 5½" tall, green mark #47
Humidor, 7" tall, green mark #47

Plate 191

Humidor, 7½" tall, green mark #47

Plate 186

Plate 187

Plate 188

Plate 189

Plate 190

Plate 191

Plate 192

Top Row:
> Pair of vases, both 8¾" high, blue mark #89

Middle Row:
> Vase, 6" tall, blue mark #52
> Vase, 9" tall, unmarked

Bottom Row:
> Vase, 8¾" tall, blue mark #52
> Vase, 8¼" tall, blue mark #52

Plate 193

> Vase, 9" tall, blue mark #52
> Vase, 8¾" tall, green mark #47

Plate 194

> Vase, 6½" tall, green mark #52
> Basket vase, 10" tall, blue mark #52

Plate 195

> Ewer, 9¼" tall, blue mark #89
> Vase, 5¼" tall, blue mark #52

Plate 196

> Vase, 9¼" tall, blue mark #47
> Vase, 9" tall, green mark #52

Plate 192

Plate 193

Plate 194

Plate 195

Plate 196

143

Plate 197

Top Row:
    Vase, 7½" tall, blue mark #52
    Vase, 7½" tall, green mark #52
Middle Row:
    Vase, 10½" tall, blue mark #52
Bottom Row:
    Vase, 10½" tall, blue mark #52
    Vase, 9" tall, unmarked

Plate 198

    Vase, 8¾" tall, blue mark #52
    Vase, 11" tall, blue mark #4

Plate 199

    Vase, 7½" tall, unmarked
    Vase, 9" tall, blue mark #52

Plate 200

    Vase, 6" tall, green mark #47
    Vase, 6¾" tall, blue mark #52
    Vase, 6" tall, green mark #47

Plate 201

    Vase, 6½" tall, blue mark #52

Plate 198

Plate 197

Plate 199

Plate 200

Plate 201

Plate 202

Top Row:

      Vase, 10¾" tall, green mark #47

      Vase, 9½" tall, green mark #47

      Vase, 11" tall, blue mark #47

Middle Row:

      Vase, 6¾" tall, green mark #47

      Vase, 7¼" tall, blue mark #71

      Vase, 6¾" tall, green mark #47

Bottom Row:

      Vase, 6¾" tall, green mark #47

      Vase, 7" tall, green mark #47

      Vase, 6¾" tall, green mark #47

Plate 203

      Vase, 12" tall, blue mark #38

Plate 204

      Vase, 5½" tall, green mark #47

Plate 205

      Vase, 8½" tall, gold mark #47

      Vase, 9" tall, green mark #91

Plate 206

      Vase, 5½" tall, blue mark #52

Plate 203

Plate 204

Plate 202

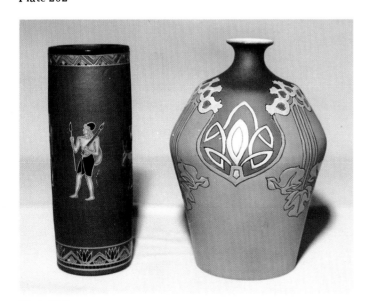

Plate 205

Plate 206

Plate 207

Top Row:
    Pair of vases, 10 " high, green mark #52
Middle Row:
    Pair of vases, 9" high, green mark #47
Bottom Row:
    Pair of vases, 8½" high, blue mark #52

Plate 208

    Urn, 16½" tall, green mark #47

Plate 209

    Pair of vases, 6¼" tall, green mark #47

Plate 210

    Pair of vases, 9¼" tall, green mark #47

Plate 208

Plate 207

Plate 209

Plate 210

149

Plate 211

Top Row:
    Ewer, 9½" tall, blue mark #89
    Vase, 8" tall, green mark #47
Middle Row:
    Vase, 9¾" high, green mark #47
Bottom Row:
    Vase, 6¾" tall, green mark #47
    Vase, 6½" tall, blue mark #52

Plate 212

    Vase, 10¾" tall, green mark #47

Plate 213

    Vase, 8½" tall, green mark #47

Plate 214

    Pair of vases, 11" tall, green mark #47

Plate 215

    Pair of vases, 7¾" tall, blue mark #52

Plate 212

Plate 213

Plate 211

Plate 214

Plate 215

151

Plate 216

Top Row:
      Vase, 9¾" tall, green mark #47
      Vase, 9¾" tall, green mark #47
Middle Row:
      Vase, 8½" tall, green mark #52
Bottom Row:
      Vase, 10" tall, blue mark #52
      Vase, 9¼" tall, green mark #52

Plate 217

Bottle vase, 10¼" tall, blue mark #52

Plate 218

Vase, 10" tall, blue mark #52

Plate 219

Vase, 7" tall, unmarked
Vase, 6½" tall, blue mark #52

Plate 220

Vase, 8¾" tall, blue mark #52

Plate 217

Plate 218

Plate 216

Plate 219

Plate 220

Plate 221

Top Row:
      Vase, 9½" tall, green mark #47
      Vase, 6½" tall, green mark #47
      Vase, 10½" tall, green mark #47
Middle Row:
      Vase, 7" tall, green mark #47
      Vase, 6" tall, blue mark #52
Bottom Row:
      Vase, 8¼" tall, green mark #47
      Vase, 8¼" tall, blue mark #52

Plate 222

Top Row:
      Vase, 7" tall, green mark #47
Bottom Row:
      Vase, 6" tall, green mark #47

Plate 223

      Vase, 8½" tall, green mark #47
      Vase, 12" tall, blue mark #38
      Vase, 8" tall, green mark #47

Plate 224

      Vase, 12" tall, green mark #52

Plate 221

Plate 222

Plate 223

Plate 224

Plate 225

Top Row:
    Vase, 9½" tall, blue mark #52
    Vase, 9½" tall, blue mark #89
Middle Row:
    Vase, 5¾" tall, green mark #47
Bottom Row:
    Vase, 8½" tall, green mark #47
    Vase, 9½" tall, green mark #47

Plate 226

    Vase, 11" tall, green mark #52

Plate 227

    Ewer, 7¼" tall, blue mark #52
    Ewer, 7¼" tall, green mark #47

Plate 228

    Vase, 9¾" tall, green mark #47
    Vase, 9¾" tall, blue mark #47

Plate 226

Plate 225

Plate 227

Plate 228

157

Plate 229

Top Row:
Vase, 8¾" tall, green mark #47
Vase, 6¾" tall, blue mark #106
Vase, 9" tall, green mark #52
Middle Row:
Vase, 5½" tall, blue mark #52
Vase, 3½" tall, blue mark #52
Vase, 5¼" tall, blue mark #47
Bottom Row:
Vase, 7¼" tall, green mark #47
Vase, 8" tall, blue mark #52
Vase, 7¼" tall, blue mark #52

Plate 230

Vase, 14" tall, red mark #4

Plate 231

Vase, 11" tall, green mark #52
Vase, 9¾" tall, green mark #4

Plate 232

Vase, 14" tall, blue mark #47

Plate 230

Plate 229

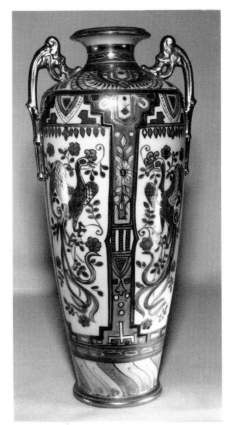

Plate 231

Plate 232

Plate 233

Lamp, 17" tall to top of socket, mark unknown

Plate 234

Candle lamp, 12½" tall, green mark #47

Plate 235

Night light, two pieces, top lifts off at bottom of apron, has glass eyes, 6½" tall, green mark #47

Plate 236

Lamp, 18" to end of fixture, green mark #47

Plate 237

Lamp, 16" tall to top of socket, green mark #52

Plate 233

Plate 234

Plate 235

Plate 236

Plate 237

Plate 238

Punch bowl, also could be used as large fruit compote, 10" wide, 6¾" high, green mark #47

Plate 239

Banquet size punch bowl, 12¾" high, 13" wide including handles, green mark #47

Plate 240

Punch bowl, also could be used as large fruit compote, 6¾" high, 12" wide including handles, green mark #47

Plate 241

Punch bowl, also could be used as large fruit compote, 6¾" high, 12" wide including handles, green mark #47

Plate 242

Matching chocolate set consisting of pot and four cups and saucers, pot measures 9" in height, all have green mark #47

Plate 238

Plate 239

Plate 240

Plate 241

Plate 242

Plate 243

Ferner, 7" long, green mark #47
Ferner, 8" long, green mark #47
Ferner, 7" long, green mark #52

Plate 244

Ferner, 5¾" wide, blue mark #84
Ferner, 6" wide, blue mark #52
Ferner, 5¾" wide, blue mark #52

Plate 245

Top Row:
Ferner, 7¼" wide, blue mark #52
Ferner, 4½" wide, blue mark #52
Ferner, 8" wide including handles #52
Bottom Row:
Ferner, 7¼" wide, blue mark #52
Ferner, 6½" wide, blue mark #52
Ferner, 7½" wide, blue mark #52

Plate 246

Ferner, 9½" wide including handles, green mark #47
Ferner, 8" long, green mark #47

Plate 247

Ferner, 8" long, blue mark #52
Ferner, 8" long, green mark #47

Plate 243

Plate 244

Plate 245

Plate 246

Plate 247

Plate 248

Nut set, large bowl is 7½" wide, small ones are 3½" wide, blue mark #52

Plate 249

Nut set, large bowl is 7½" wide, mark #75, small bowls are 3" wide and marked with green mark #81

Plate 250

Nut set, large bowl is 6¾" wide, small bowls are 3" wide, green mark #47

Plate 251

Nut set, large bowl is 10½" wide, small bowls are 3" wide, mark #80

Plate 252

Nut set, large bowl is 9½" wide, small bowls are 3¾" wide, red mark #47

Plate 248

Plate 249

Plate 250

Plate 251

Plate 252

Plate 253

Nut set, large bowl is 7" wide, small bowls are 3" wide, all are marked with blue mark #47

Plate 254

Nut set, large bowl is 7½" wide, small bowls are 3" wide, blue mark #52

Plate 255

Handled nappy 7" wide, green mark #47
Sauce dish, 7" long, blue mark #52

Plate 256

Bowl, 7¼" wide, blue mark #52
Three compartment dish, 7½" wide, green mark #47

Plate 257

Bowl, 10" wide, green mark #47
Bowl, 7" wide, green mark #47

Plate 258

Three handled bowl, 7" wide, green mark #47
Bowl, 7¾" wide, green mark #47

Plate 253

Plate 254

Plate 255

Plate 257

Plate 256

Plate 258

169

Plate 259

Three legged bowl, 7¼" wide, green mark #47
Three legged bowl, 7¼" wide, green mark #47

Plate 260

Bowl, 6¼" wide, blue mark #84
Handled nappy, 6½" wide, green mark #47

Plate 261

Two handled bowl, 6¼" wide, green mark #47
Relish dish, 7¾" long, blue mark #52

Plate 262

Two handled bowl, 9½" wide, blue mark #52
Bowl, 8¾" wide, green mark #47

Plate 263

Bowl, 8" wide, unmarked
Two handled bowl, 7½" wide, green mark #47

Plate 259

Plate 260

Plate 261

Plate 262

Plate 263

Plate 264

Bowl, 9¾" wide, blue mark #52
Bowl, 9¾" wide, mark #80

Plate 265

Bowl, 7¾" long, blue mark #84
Bowl, 7½" long, green mark #47

Plate 266

Bowl, 8½" wide, green mark #47
Bowl, 9½" long, green mark #47

Plate 267

Bowl, 9" in diameter, red mark #96

Plate 268

Bowl, 7½" in diameter, green mark #47
Bowl, 7¾" wide, green mark #47

Plate 269

Bowl, 8" in diameter, blue mark #52

Plate 264

Plate 265

Plate 266

Plate 267

Plate 268

Plate 269

Plate 270

Bowl, 7" wide, green mark #47
Bowl, 6½" wide, green mark #47
Bowl, 6" wide, green mark #47

Plate 271

Bowl, 11½" wide, green mark #47
Footed bowl, 8" in diameter, blue mark #52

Plate 272

Bowl, 10" wide, green mark #47

Plate 273

Bowl, molded in low relief, 7" wide, green mark #47

Plate 274

Nut bowl, 5¾" wide, blue mark #52

Plate 275

Sugar shaker, 4" tall, blue mark #52
Covered pancake server, 8¾" in diameter, red mark #47
Sugar shaker, 4" tall, blue mark #52

Plate 276

Top Row:
Bowl, 9" long, green mark #47
Bottom Row:
Bowl, 6¾" wide, green mark #47

Plate 270

Plate 271

Plate 272

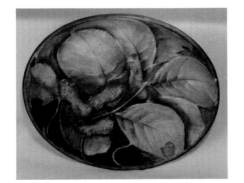

Plate 273

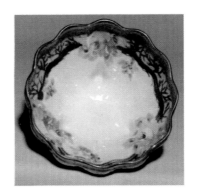

Plate 274

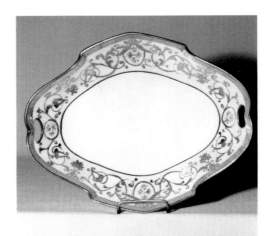

Plate 275

Plate 276

Plate 277

Top Row:

Sugar shaker, 4" tall, green mark #52
Spoonholder, 7¾" long, blue mark #52
Napkin ring, 2" long, green mark #47
Gravy boat with underplate, underplate is 6" long, mark #80

Bottom Row:

Cinnamon stick holder, 4½" tall, blue mark #52
Sugar shaker, 4¾" tall, green mark #47
Trivet, 5" square, green mark #47
Incense burner, 3¼" tall, red mark #14
Sugar shaker, 4¾" tall, unmarked

Plate 278

Top Row:

Three dutch shoes, all 3" long, all have green mark #47
Talcum powder flask, 5" tall, blue mark #84
Three napkin rings, all 2" long, all have green mark #47

Bottom Row:

Inkwell with pen rest, 3½" high, has inner well, mark #80
Inkwell with inner well, 3" square, green mark #47
Novelty face, 4¼" wide, blue mark #84
Heart shaped cigar holder and tray, blue mark #52
Oval shaped cigar holder and tray, green mark #47

Plate 277

Plate 278

177

Plate 279

Top Row:

    Lemon dish, 5½" wide, blue mark #84

    Three handled toothpick holder, 2¼" tall, green mark #47

    Plate, 6¼" in diameter, green mark #47

Middle Row:

    Egg cup, 2½" tall, green mark #47

    Nut cup, scene of three geisha girls in old fashioned car, 2¾" in diameter, green mark #101

    Cup, 3¼" tall, green mark #81

Bottom Row:

    Coaster, 3¾" in diameter, blue mark #84

    Trivet, 6¼" wide, green mark #47

    Coaster, 3¾" in diameter, green mark #47

Plate 280

Top Row:

    Mustache cup and saucer, blue mark #84

    Mustache cup and saucer, blue mark #84

Bottom Row:

    Coaster, 3¾" in diameter, green mark #47

    Shaving cup, 3¾" tall, green mark #47

    Coaster, 3¾" in diameter, blue mark #52

Plate 281

Top Row:

    Pair of salt and pepper shakers, blue mark #94

    Individual salt, green mark #47

    Pair of salt and pepper shakers, blue mark #52

Middle Row:

    Individual salt, green mark #52

    Pair of salt and pepper shakers, unmarked

    Master salt, green mark #47

Bottom Row:

    Pair of salt and pepper shakers, blue mark #55

    Pair of salt and pepper shakers in holder, blue mark #84

    Pair of salt and pepper shakers, green mark #26

Plate 279

Plate 280

Plate 281

179

Plate 282

Top Row:

Pitcher, 5½" tall, blue mark #52

Pitcher, 7" tall, blue mark #81

Covered pitcher, 7" tall, blue mark #52

Bottom Row:

Pitcher, 7" tall, green mark #52

Pitcher, 7" tall, blue mark #52

Plate 283

Top Row:

Pancake server, 8¾" in diameter, mark #80

Pancake server, 8¾" in diameter, blue mark #52

Pancake server, 8¾" in diameter, green mark #47

Bottom Row:

Butter dish, 7½" in diameter, green mark #47

Butter dish, 7¾" in diameter, mark #80

Cheese and cracker dish, 8½" in diameter, blue mark #52

Plate 282

Plate 283

181

Plate 284

Top Row:

Bouillon cup, 3¾" diameter, green mark #81

Covered bouillon cup with underplate, 5" tall, green mark #52

Middle Row:

Knife rest, 3¾" long, green mark #47

Butter pat, 3¾" in diameter, blue mark #84

Bottom Row:

Egg warmer, 5½" in diameter, green mark #47

Egg cup, 2½" tall, blue mark #84

Plate 285

All six items have green mark #47. Individual chocolate pot is 5¾" tall.

Individual coffeepot is 6¼" tall

Egg cup is 2½" tall

Creamer is 2½" tall

Pair of salt and pepper shakers are 2¾" tall

Plate 286

Top Row:

Condensed milk container, 6" tall, blue mark #52

Condensed milk container, 6" tall, mark #80

Bottom Row:

Jam jar with underplate, 6" tall, blue mark #52

Condensed milk container, 6¼" tall, blue mark #52

Plate 287

Top Row:

Tea strainer, top piece is 6" long, blue mark #52

Tea strainer, 6" long, unmarked

Middle Row:

Tea strainer, 6" long, unmarked

Tea strainer, 6" long, unmarked

Bottom Row:

Tea strainer, 5" long, blue mark #52

Tea strainer, 6" long, green mark #47

Plate 284

Plate 285

Plate 286

Plate 287

Plate 288

Top Row:
    Syrup, 5¾" tall, green mark #47
    Syrup, 4½" tall, green mark #47
Bottom Row:
    Syrup, 5" tall, blue mark #52
    Handled, individual coffeepot, 5¾" tall, blue mark #81
    Syrup, 4" tall, green mark #47

Plate 289

    Lemonade pitcher, 6" tall, blue mark #52
    Lemonade cups, 3¾" tall, blue mark #7

Plate 290

    Slanted cheese dish, 7¾" long, magenta mark # 47

Plate 291

    Lazy susan in papier mache box, 12" in diameter, green mark #7

Plate 292

    Individual condiment set, tray is 4¼" wide, mustard, salt and pepper shakers, blue mark #84
    Condiment set, tray is 7" wide, mustard jar, toothpick holder, salt and pepper shakers, magenta mark #47

Plate 288

Plate 289

Plate 290

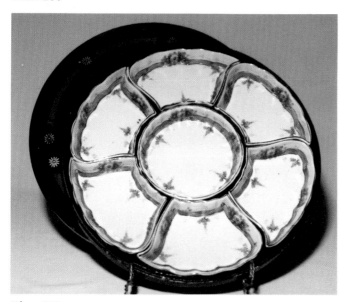

Plate 291

Plate 292

Plate 293

Four bouillon cups with saucers, blue mark #52

Plate 294

Top Row:
Mustard jar, 3½" tall, blue mark #84
Mustard jar, 3" tall, green mark #47
Bottom Row:
Mustard jar, 3¼" tall, blue mark #52
Mustard jar, 3¾" tall, green mark #81

Plate 295

Potpourri jar with inner lid, 5½" tall, green mark #47
Covered jar, 4½" tall, red mark #100

Plate 296

Bell shaped match holder and striker, 3½" tall, green mark #47

Plate 297

Covered jar, 5½" tall, green mark #47

Plate 298

Covered jar, 6" tall, green mark #47
Covered jar, 4¾" tall, blue mark #52
Covered jar, 6½" tall, green mark #47

Plate 293

Plate 294

Plate 295

Plate 296

Plate 297

Plate 298

187

Plate 299

Celery set with six salts, dish is 13" long, all are backstamped with the green mark #47

Plate 300

Relish set with six salts, dish is 8¼" long, mark #109

Plate 301

Celery dish, 12" long, green mark #47

Plate 302

Celery set with six salts, dish is 12½" long, all are marked with mark #80

Plate 303

Handled relish dish having two compartments, 7½" long, blue mark #52
Relish dish, 9½" long, blue mark #52

Plate 299

Plate 300

Plate 301

Plate 302

Plate 303

Plate 304

Top Row:
    Sugar and creamer set, green mark #47
Bottom Row:
    Sugar and creamer set, red mark #110

Plate 305

    Sugar and creamer set with matching handled dish. Dish is 7¾" wide, all
    have green mark #47

Plate 306

Top Row:
    Sugar bowl, blue mark #52
    Creamer, green mark #81
    Sugar bowl, green mark #47
Bottom Row:
    Sugar and creamer set, green mark #47

Plate 307

Top Row:
    Sugar and creamer set, mark #80
Bottom Row:
    Sugar and creamer set, green mark #4

Plate 304

Plate 305

Plate 306

Plate 307

191

Plate 308

Cracker jar, 9½" wide including handles, green mark #47
Matching bowl, 7½" long, green mark #47

Plate 309

Cracker jar, 8½" wide including handles, unmarked
Dish, 6½" wide, blue mark #52

Plate 310

Cookie jar, 7½" tall, green mark #47
Cookie jar, 6¾" tall, red mark #4

Plate 311

Cookie jar, 8¼" tall, red mark #100

Plate 312

Cracker jar, 9½" wide, unmarked
Cracker jar, 9" wide, green mark #47

Plate 308

Plate 309

Plate 311

Plate 310

Plate 312

Plate 313

Top Row:
Cup and saucer, green mark #47
Scenic cup and saucer, mark #109
Bottom Row:
Cup and saucer, blue mark #81
Cup and saucer, blue mark #44
Cup and saucer, blue mark #47

Plate 314

Pieces from a luncheon set
Top Row:
Nut cup, red mark #47
Sugar and creamer set, green mark #47
Covered trinket box, green mark #47
Sugar shaker, green mark #47
Bottom Row:
Matchbox holder, red mark #47
Two small bowls, red mark #47
Large bowl, 9½" wide, red mark #47
Two coasters, red mark #47

Plate 315

Bowl, 6¾" wide including handles, green mark #47
Bowl, 7¼" wide, blue mark #47
Covered trinket box, green mark #47
Compote, green mark #47

Plate 316

Loving cup vase, 5½" tall, green mark #47

Plate 313

Plate 314

Plate 315

Plate 316

Plate 317

Chocolate set, pot is 8½" tall, cake plate is 11¼" in diameter, candy dish is 9¼" long, set contains six cups and saucers, all pieces have green mark #47

Plate 318

Fish set, platter is 22½" long and 9½" wide, set comes with 12 8½" plates, gravy bowl with underplate which is 8¼" long and ladle. All pieces have green mark #47

Plate 317

Plate 318

Plate 319

Chocolate set, pot is 11" tall and set contains four cups and saucers, green mark #79

Plate 320

Demitasse set, tray is 12" in diameter, pot is 6" tall, creamer and sugar bowl, four cups and saucers, blue mark #84

Plate 319

Plate 320

Plate 321

Tea set, pot is 5" tall, set has sugar bowl, creamer and four cups and saucers, all pieces are marked with blue mark #72

Plate 322

Tea set, pot is 7½" tall, set contains sugar bowl, creamer and four cups and saucers all have green mark #50

Plate 321

Plate 322   201

Plate 323

Tea set, teapot is 5" tall, blue mark #52

Plate 324

Tea set, teapot is 7" tall, blue mark #71

Plate 325

Compote, 8½" in diameter including handles, blue mark #52
Compote, 8½" in diameter, blue mark #52
Compote, 9½" in diameter including handles, blue mark #52

Plate 326

Snack set, tray is 8½" long, magenta mark #96

Plate 327

Snack set, tray is 8½" long, blue mark #52

Plate 328

Top Row:
Bowl, 8" long, mark #80
Bowl, 7¾" wide, unmarked
Bottom Row:
Creamer and sugar set, green mark #81
Bowl, 9¼" in diameter, blue mark #81

Plate 323

Plate 324

Plate 325

Plate 326

Plate 327

Plate 328

Plate 329

Top Row:

Bowl, 8½" wide including handles, green mark #47
Bowl, 8½" wide, green mark #47

Bottom Row:

Sugar and creamer set, green mark #47
Small bowl, 7¾" wide, green mark #47

Plate 330

Top Row:

Pair of chambersticks, 6" in diameter, green mark #52

Bottom Row:

Pair of candlesticks, 8" tall, green mark #47
Candlestick, 9" tall, green mark #47

Plate 329

Plate 330

205

Plate 331

Top Row:

Trinket box, blue mark #52

Trinket box, green mark #47

Middle Row:

Trinket box, blue mark #52

Trinket box, blue mark #52

Bottom Row:

Trinket box, blue mark #47

Trinket box, green mark #47

Plate 332

Top Row:

Trinket box, blue mark #52

Trinket box, magenta mark #47

Middle Row:

Trinket box, 4" long, green mark #47

Bottom Row:

Jewelry box, 4¾" wide, green mark #47

Plate 333

Top Row:

Hatpin holder, 4¾" tall, mark #80

Middle Row:

Hatpin holder, 4¾" tall, blue mark #52

Hatpin holder, 4½" tall green mark #52

Bottom Row:

Hatpin holder, 4½" tall, blue mark #47

Hatpin holder, 4½" tall, green mark #81

Plate 334

Top Row:

Hatpin holder with attached underplate, 4¼" tall, blue mark #47

Hatpin holder with attached underplate, 4½" tall, green mark #52

Bottom Row:

Hatpin holder with attached underplate, 4½" tall, blue mark #52

Plate 335

Hatpin holder, 4¾" tall, woodland scene, blue mark #52

Plate 336

Top Row:

Vanity organizer, combination hatpin holder and ring tree with attached underplate, 4¼" tall, magenta mark #4

Ring holder, 2½" tall, blue mark #52

Middle Row:

Stickpin holder, 1½" tall, green mark #47

Bottom Row:

Ring holder, 3" tall, blue mark #84

Hanging hatpin holder, 7" long, blue mark #52

Plate 331

Plate 332

Plate 333

Plate 334

Plate 335

Plate 336

207

Plate 337

Powder box, 5½" wide, green mark #47
Footed powder box, 4¼" wide, green mark #47

Plate 338

Compote, 5" high, mark #80
Powder box, 3¾" wide, green mark #116

Plate 339

Hair receiver, 5" wide, blue mark #52
Hair receiver, 5¼" wide, blue mark #52
Hair receiver, 4½" wide, green mark #52

Plate 340

Hair receiver, 4½" wide, unmarked
Hair receiver, 5" wide, mark #37
Hair receiver, 5" wide, green mark #47

Plate 341

Dresser set, tray is 10" long, consists of hair receiver, hatpin holder, powder box and compote, tray is marked with blue mark #52, other pieces are green mark #47

Plate 342

Hair receiver, 4½" wide, green mark #52
Hair receiver, 4¾" long, green mark #47
Hair receiver, 4" in diameter, blue mark #52

Plate 343

Top Row:
Matching hair receiver and powder box, 4" wide, green mark #47
Middle Row:
Matching hair receiver and powder box, 4½" wide, green mark #52
Bottom Row:
Matching hair receiver and small dish, hair receiver is 4½" wide and dish is 5½" wide, mark #80

Plate 344

Cologne bottle, 5¼" tall, green mark #47
Cologne bottle, 5" tall, green mark #47

Plate 337

Plate 339

Plate 338

Plate 340

Plate 341

Plate 342

Plate 343

Plate 344

209

Plate 345

Top Row:

      Hanging matchbox holder, 4½" long, green mark #47

      Ashtray, 5" in diameter, green mark #47

      Ashtray, 5½" wide, green mark #47

      Ashtray, 4½" wide, green mark #47

      Matchbox holder, green mark #26

Bottom Row:

      Matchbox holder with attached tray, 4" long, green mark #47

      Spitoon, 3¼" in diameter, green mark #47

      Cigar ashtray, 4¾" wide, green mark #47

      Spitoon, 3¼" in diameter, blue mark #52

      Ashtray, 5½" long, green mark #47

Plate 346

Top Row:

      Ashtray, 5½" wide, green mark #47

      Hanging matchbox holder, 4½" long, green mark #47

      Ashtray, 4¾" long, green mark #47

      Ashtray, 4½" wide, green mark #47

Bottom Row:

      Ashtray, 5" in diameter, green mark #47

      Set of four coasters, 3½" in diameter, all green mark #47

      Ashtray, 5" wide, blue mark #47

      Ashtray, 5" wide, green mark #47

Plate 345

Plate 346

211

Plate 347

Top Row:

Cigarette box, 4¾" long, green mark #47

Cigarette box, 4½" long, blue mark #47

Middle Row:

Cigarette box, signed with dog's name, Champion Katerfelto, 5½" long, green mark #47

Cigarette box, 5½" long, green mark #47

Bottom Row:

Cigarette box, 4¼" long, green mark #47

Cigarette box, 4¼" long, green mark #47

Plate 348

Top Row:

Ink blotter, 4¼" long, green mark #47

Inkwell, 4" wide, green mark #47

Bottom Row:

Inkwell, 2¼" wide, green mark #47

Stamp box, inside has two compartments, 2¾" long, green mark #47

Plate 349

Five piece smoke set with a large humidor to match. Large humidor is 6" tall, all have green mark #47

Plate 347

Plate 348

Plate 349

213

Plate 350

Cake plate, 10½" wide, green and red mark #10
Cake plate, 10½" wide, blue mark #47
Cake plate, 9¾" wide, blue mark #47

Plate 351

Bread tray, 14¼" long, green mark #47
Cake plate, 11" wide, green mark #52

Plate 352

Plate, 8½" wide, green mark #47
Plate, 8¾" wide, green mark #52

Plate 353

Plate, 7½" wide, blue mark #52
Plate, 7½" wide, green mark #47

Plate 354

Dinner plate, 10¼" wide, green mark #47
Plate, 8¾" wide, blue mark #52

Plate 350

Plate 351

Plate 352

Plate 353

Plate 354

215

Plate 355

Hanging placque, 10" wide, blue mark #52
Hanging placque, 9" wide, blue mark #52

Plate 356

Hanging placque, 10" wide, blue mark #52

Plate 357

Hanging placque, 10" wide, green mark #47
Hanging placque, 10" wide, blue mark #47

Plate 358

Hanging placque, 10" wide, green mark #47

Plate 359

Hanging placque, 10" wide, green mark #47
Hanging placque, 9" wide, blue mark #47

Plate 360

Hanging placque, 11½" wide, blue mark #52

Plate 355

Plate 356

Plate 357

Plate 358

Plate 359

Plate 360

217

Plate 361

Hanging placque, 10¼" long x 8" wide, green mark #47
Hanging placque, 10¼" long x 8" wide, green mark #47
Hanging placque, 10¼" long x 8" wide, green mark #47

Plate 362

Hanging placque, 10" wide, green mark #47

Plate 363

Hanging placque, 10½" wide, green mark #47
Hanging placque, 10½" wide, green mark #47
Hanging placque, 10½" wide, green mark #47

Plate 364

Hanging placque, 10" wide, blue mark #52

Plate 365

Hanging placque, 8¾" wide, green mark #47
Hanging placque, 7¾" wide, green mark #47
Hanging placque, 9" wide, green mark #52

Plate 366

Large hanging placque (charger), 14" wide, green mark #47

Plate 361

Plate 362

Plate 363

Plate 364

Plate 365

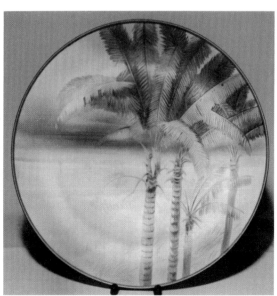

Plate 366

GLOSSARY

American Indian design — a popular collectible in Nippon porcelain, these designs include the Indian in a canoe, Indian warrior, Indian hunting wild game and the Indian maiden.

Apricot (ume)   in Japan, stands for strength and nobility, is also a symbol of good luck.

Art Deco — a style of decoration which hit its peak in Europe and America around 1925 although items were manufactured with this decor as early as 1910. The style was modernistic. Geometric patterns were popular. Motifs used were shapes such as circles, rectangles, cylinders and cones.

Art Nouveau — the name is derived from the French words meaning new art. During the period of 1885-1925 artists tended to use bolder colors and realism was rejected. Free flowing designs were used, breaking away from the imitations of the past.

Artist signed — items signed by the artist, most appear to be of English extraction probably painted during the hey-day of hand painting chinaware at the turn of the century.

Azalea pattern — pattern found on Nippon items, pink azaleas with green to gray leaves and gold rims. Nippon marked pieces match the Noritake marked azalea pattern items. The Azalea pattern was originally offered by the Larkin Co. to its customers as premiums.

Backstamp — mark found on Nippon porcelain items identifying the manufacturer, exporter or importer and country of origin.

Bamboo tree — symbolic of strength, faithfulness and honesty in Japan, also a good luck symbol. The bamboo resists the storm but it yields to it and rises again.

Beading — generally a series of clay dots applied on Nippon porcelain, very often enameled over in gold. Later Nippon pieces merely had dots of enameling.

Blank — greenware or bisque items devoid of decoration.

Blown-out items — this term is used by collectors and dealers for items that have a molded relief pattern embossed on by the mold in which the article was shaped. It is not actually "blown-out" as glass items are, but the pattern is raised up from the background of the item. (See Molded Relief)

Biscuit — clay which has been fired but unglazed.

Bisque — same as biscuit, term also used by collectors to describe a matte finish on an item.

Böttger, Johanne, F. — a young German alchemist who supposedly discovered the value of kaolin in making porcelain. This discovery helped to revolutionize the china making industry in Europe beginning in the early 1700's.

Carp — fish that symbolizes strength and perseverance.

Casting — the process of making reproductions by pouring slip into molds.

Cha no yu — Japanese tea ceremony.

Chargers — archaic term for large platters or plates.

Cheese hard clay — same as leather hard clay.

Cherry blossoms — national flower of Japan and emblem of the faithful warrior.

Ching-tê-Chên — ancient city in China where nearly a million people lived and worked with almost all devoted to the making of porcelain.

Chrysanthamum — depicts health and longevity, the crest of the Emperor of Japan. The chrysanthamum blooms late in the year and lives longer than other flowers.

Citron — stands for wealth.

Cloisonné on Porcelain — on Nippon porcelain wares it resembles the other cloisonné pieces except that it was produced on a porcelain body instead of metal. The decoration is divided into cells called cloisons. These cloisons are divided by strips of metal wire which kept the colors separated during the firing.

Cobalt oxide — blue oxide imported to Japan after 1868 for decoration of wares. Gosu, a pebble found in Oriental riverbeds had previously been used but was scarce and more expensive than the imported oxide. Cobalt oxide is the most powerful of all the coloring oxides for tinting.

Coralene items — were made by firing small colored beads on the wares. Most are signed Kinran, US Patent, NBR 912171, February 9, 1909, Japan. Tiny glass beads had previously been applied to glass items in the shapes of birds, flowers, leaves, etc. and no doubt this was an attempt to copy it. Japanese coralene was patented by Alban L. Rock, an American living in Yokohama, Japan. The vitreous coating of beads gave the item a plush velvety look. The beads were permanently fired on and gave a luminesence to the design. The most popular design had been one of seaweed and coral hence the name *coralene* was given to this type of design.

Crane — a symbol of good luck in Japan, also stands for marital fidelity and is an emblem of longevity.

Daffadil — a sign of spring to the Japanese.

Decalcomania — a process of transferring a wet paper print onto the surface of an item. It was made to resemble hand painted work.

Deer — stands for divine messenger.

Diaper pattern — repetitive pattern of small design used on Nippon porcelain, often geometric or floral.

Dragons (ryu) — a symbol of strength, goodness and good fortune. The Japanese dragon has three claws and was thought to reside in the sky. Clouds, water and lightening often accompany the dragon. The dragon is often portrayed in high relief using the slip trailing method of decor.

Drain mold — a mold used in making hollow ware. Liquid slip is poured into the mold until the desired thickness of the walls is achieved. The excess clay is poured out. When the item starts to shrink away from the mold, it is removed.

Drape mold — or flopover mold, used to make flat bottomed items. Moist clay is rolled out and draped over the mold. It is then pressed firmly into shape.

Dutch scenes — popular on Nippon items, include those of windmills, and men and women dressed in Dutch costumes.

Edo — or Yedo, the largest city in Japan, later renamed Tokyo, meaning eastern capitol.

Embossed design — see molded relief.

Enamel beading — dots of enameling painted by the artist in gold or other colors and often made to resemble jewels such as emeralds and rubies. Many times this raised beading will be found in brown or black colors.

Fairings — items won or bought at fairs as a souvenir of the event.

Feldspar — most common rock found on earth.

Fern Leaves — symbolic of ample good fortune.

Fettles or Mold Marks — ridges formed where sections of molds are joined at the seam. These fettles have to be removed before the item is decorated.

Finial — the top knob on a cover of an item, used to lift the cover off.

Firing — the cooking or baking of clay ware.

Flopover mold — same as a drape mold.

Flux — an ingredient added to glaze to assist in making the item fire properly. It causes the glaze to melt at a specified temperature.

Glaze — composed of silica, alumina and flux, and is applied to porcelain pieces. During the firing process the glaze joins together with the clay item to form a glasslike surface. It seals the pores and makes the item impervious to liquids.

Gold trim — has to be fired at lower temperatures or the gold would sink into the enameled decoration. If overfired, the gold becomes discolored.

Gouda ceramics — originally made in Gouda, a province of South Holland. These items were copied on the Nippon wares and were patterned after the Art Nouveau style.

Gosu — pebble found in Oriental riverbeds, a natural cobalt. It was used to color items until 1868 when oxidized cobalt was introduced into Japan.

Greenware — clay which has been molded but not fired.

Hard paste porcelain — paste meaning the body of substance, porcelain being made from clay using kaolin. This produces a hard translucent body when fired.

Hō-ō bird — sort of a bird of paradise who resides on earth and is associated with the Empress of Japan. Also see phoenix bird.

Incised backstamp — the backstamp marking is scratched into the surface of a clay item.

Incised deocration — a sharp tool or stick was used to produce the design right onto the body of the article while it was still in a state of soft clay.

Iris — the Japanese believe this flower wards off evil, it is associated with warriors because of its sword like leaves.

Jasper Ware — see Wedgewood.

Jigger — a machine resembling a potter's wheel. Soft pliable clay is placed onto a convex revolving mold. As the wheel turns, a template is held against it trimming off the excess clay on the outside. The revolving mold shapes the inside of the item and the template cuts the outside.

Jolley — a machine like a jigger only in reverse. The revolving mold is concave and the template forms the inside of the item. The template is lowered inside the revolving mold. The mold forms the outside surface while the template cuts the inside.

Jōmon — neolithic hunters and fishermen in Japan dating back to approximately 2500 B.C. Their pottery was hand formed and marked with an overall rope or cord pattern. It was made of unwashed clay, unglazed and was baked in open fires.

Kaga — province in Japan.

Kaolin — a highly refractory clay and one of the principal ingredients used in making porcelain. It is a pure white residual clay, a decomposition of granite.

Kao-ling — a word meaning "the high hills" in Chinese, the word kaolin is derived from it.

Kiln — oven in which pottery is fired.

Leather hard clay — clay which is dry enough to hold its shape but still damp and moist, no longer in a plastic state, also called cheese hard.

Liquid slip — clay in a liquid state.

Lobster — symbol of long life.

Luster decoration — a metallic type of coloring decoration, gives an irridescent effect.

Matte finish — also referred to as mat and matt. A dull glaze having a low reflectance when fired.

McKinley Tariff Act of 1890 — Chapter 1244, Section 6 states "That on and after the first day of March, eighteen hundred and ninety-one, all articles of foreign manufacture, such as are usually or ordinarily marked, stamped, branded, or labeled, and all packages containing such or other imported articles, shall, respectively, be plainly marked, stamped, branded, or labeled in legible English words, so as to indicate the country of their origin; and unless so marked, stamped, branded, or labeled they shall not be admitted to entry".

Meiji period — period of 1868-1912 in Japan when Emperor Mutsuhito resigned. It means enlightened rule.

Middle East scenes — popular design used on Nippon pieces. They feature pyramids, deserts, palm trees and riders on camels.

Model — the shape from which the mold is made.

Molded relief items — the pattern is embossed on the item by the mold in which the article is shaped. These items give the appearance that the pattern is caused by some type of upward pressure from the underside. Collectors often refer to these items as 'blown-out'.

Molds — contain a cavity in which castings are made. They are generally made from plaster of paris and are used for shaping clay objects. Both liquid and plastic clay may be used. The mold can also be made of clay or rubber, however, plaster was generally used as it absorbs moisture immediately from the clay. Raised ornamentation may also be formed directly in the mold.

Moriage — refers to applied clay (slip) relief decoration. On Nippon items this was usually done by 'slip trailing' or hand rolling and shaping the clay on an item.

Morimura Bros. — importers of Japanese wares in the United States and the sole importers of Noritake wares. It was opened in New York City in 1876 and closed in 1941.

Mutsuhito — Emperor of Japan from 1868-1912. His reign was called the Meiji period which meant enlightened rule.

Nagoya — a large city in Japan.

Narcissus — stands for good fortune.

Ningyō — Japanese name for doll, meaning human being and image.

Nippon — the name the Japanese people called their country. It comes from a Chinese phrase meaning "the source of the sun" and sounds like Neehon in Japanese.

Noritake Co. originally registered as Nippon Gomei Kaisha. In 1917 the name was changed to Nippon Toki Kabushiki Toki. From 1918 the word Noritake appeared in conjunction with Nippon which was the designation of country of origin.

Orchid — means hidden beauty and modesty to the Japanese.

Overglaze Decoration — a design is either painted or a decal applied to an item which already has a fired glazed surface. The article is then refired to make the decoration permanent.

Pattern Stamping — the design was achieved by using a special stamp or a plaster roller having the design cut into it. The design was pressed into the soft clay body of an item.

Pauch — drink originating in India consisting of lemon juice, arrack, tea, sugar and water.

Paulownia Flower — crest of the Empress of Japan.

Peach — stands for marriage.

Peacock — stands for elegance and beauty.

Peony — considered the king of flowers in Japan.

Perry, Matthew, Comm., USN — helped to fashion the Kanagawa treaty in 1854 between the United States and Japan. This treaty opened the small ports of Shimoda and Hakodate to trade. Shipwrecked sailors were also to receive good treatment and an American Consul was permitted to reside at Shimoda.

Petuntse — clay found in felspathic rocks such as granite. Its addition to porcelain made the item more durable. Petuntse is also called china stone.

Phoenix Bird — sort of a bird of paradise which resides on earth and is associated with the Empress of Japan. This bird appears to be a cross between a peacock, a pheasant and gamecock. There appear to be many designs for this bird as each artist had his own conception as to how it should look. It is also a symbol to the Japanese of all that is beautiful.

Pickard Co. — a china decorating studio originally located in Chicago. This firm decorated blank wares imported from a number of countries including Nippon.

Pine Tree — to the Japanese this tree is symbolic of friendship and prosperity and depicts the winter season. It is also a sign of good luck and a sign of strength.

Plastic Clay — clay in a malleable state, able to be shaped and formed without collapsing.

Plum — stands for womanhood. Plum blossoms reflect bravery.

Porcelain — a mixture composed mainly of kaolin and petuntse which are fired at a high temperature and vitrified.

Porcelain Slip — porcelain clay in a liquid form.

Porcellaine — French adaption of the word porcelain.

Porcellana — Italian word meaning cowry shell. The Chinese ware which was brought back to Venice in the 15th century was thought to resemble the cowry shell and was called porcellana.

Portrait Items — items decorated with portraits, many of Victorian ladies. Some appear to be hand painted, others are decal work.

Potter's wheel — rotating device onto which a ball of plastic clay is placed. The wheel is turned and the potter molds the clay with his hands and is capable of producing cylindrical objects.

Pottery — in its broadest sense includes all forms of wares made from clay.

Press Mold — used to make handles, finials, figurines, etc. A two-piece mold into which soft clay is placed. The two pieces are pressed together to form items.

Relief — Molded (See Molded Relief Items).

Royal Ceramics — name of Nippon pieces marked with RC on backstamp.

Satsuma — a sea-going principality in Japan, an area where many of the old famous kilns are found, and also a type of Japanese ware. Satsuma is a cream colored glazed pottery which is finely crackled.

Slip — liquid clay.

Slip Trailing — a process where liquid clay was applied to porcelain via a bamboo or rubber tube. A form of painting but with clay instead of paint. The slip is often applied quite heavily and gives a thick, raised appearance.

Slurry — thick slip.

Solid Casting Mold — used for shallow type items such as bowls and plates. In this type of mold the thickness of the walls is determined by the mold and every piece is formed identical. The mold shapes both the inside and the outside of the piece and the thickness of the walls can be controlled. Solid casting can be done with either liquid or plastic clay.

Sometsuke Style Decoration — items decorated with an underglaze of blue and white colors.

Sprigging — the application of small molded relief decoration to the surface of porcelain by use of liquid clay as in Jasper Ware.

Sprig Mold — a one-piece mold used in making ornaments. Clay is fitted or poured into a mold which is incised with a design. Only one side is molded and the exposed side becomes the back of the finished item.

Taisho — name of the period reigned over by Emperor Yoshihito in Japan from 1912-1926. It means great peace.

Tapestry — a type of decor used on Nippon porcelain. A cloth was dipped into liquid slip and then stretched onto the porcelain item. During the bisque firing the material burned off and left a textured look on the porcelain piece resembling needlepoint in many cases. The item was then painted and fired again in the usual manner.

Template — profile of the pattern being cut.

Throwing — the art of forming a clay object on a potter's wheel.

Tiger (tora) — a symbol of longevity.

Transfer Print — see Decalcomania.

Translucent — not transparent but clear enough to allow rays of light to pass through.

Ultra Violet Lamp — lamp used to detect cracks and hidden repairs in items.

Underglaze decoration — this type of decoration is applied on bisque china (fired once), then the item is glazed and fired again.

Victorian Age design — decor used on some Nippon pieces, gaudy and extremely bold colors used.

Vitreous — glass-like.

Vitrify — to change into a glasslike substance due to the application of heat.

Wasters — a word for pieces ruined or marred in the kiln.

Water Lilies — represents autumn in Japan.

Wedgwood — term used to refer to Nippon pieces which attempt to imitate Josiah Wedgwood's Jasper Ware. The items generally have a light blue or green background. The Nippon pieces were produced with a slip trailing decor however, rather than the sprigging ornamentation made popular by Wedgwood. White clay slip was trailed onto the background color of the item by use of tubing to form the pattern.

Yamato — district in central Japan.

Yayoi — people of the bronze and iron culture in Japan dating back to 300-100 B.C. They were basically an agriculture people. They made pottery using the potter's wheel.

Yedo — or Edo, the largest city in Japan, renamed Tokyo meaning eastern capitol.

Yoshihito — Emperor of Japan from 1912-26. He took the name of Taisho which meant great peace.

INDEX TO NIPPON ITEMS PHOTOGRAPHED IN THE BOOK

225

Index To Information and/or Photos of Some of the Unique Patterns, Techniques and Textures Found on Nippon Items. (Also See Glossary)

BIBLIOGRAPHY

Altman, Seymour and Violet, *The Book of Buffalo Pottery*, Bonanza Books, New York, 1970.

Andacht, Sandra, *Moriage*, The Antique Trader Weekly, Dubuque, Iowa, Dec. 28, 1977.

Athearn, Robert G., *The Gilded Age*, Vol. 11 of the American Heritage, Dell Publishing Co., New York City, 1963.

Athearn, Robert G., *Age of Steel*, Vol. 10 of the American Heritage, Dell Publishing Co., New York City, 1963.

Bauer, Helen and Carlquist, Sherwin, *Japanese Festivals*, Doubleday and Co., Garden City, N.Y. 1965.

Bergamini, David, *Japan's Imperial Conspiracy*, Vol. 1, William Morrow and Co., Inc., 1971.

Boardman, Fon W., Jr., *America and the Gilded Age 1876-1900*, Henry Z. Walck, Inc., 1972.

Chaffers, William, *Collector's Handbook of Marks and Monograms on Pottery and Porcelain*, edited by Frederick Lichfield, Borden Publishing Co., Alhambra, Calif.

Cole, Ann Kilborn, *The Golden Guide to American Antiques*, Golden Press, New York, 1967.

Coleman, Dorothy S., Elizabeth A. and Evelyn J., *The Collector's Encyclopedia of Dolls*, Crown Publishers, New York City, 1968.

Conrad, John W., *Ceramic Formulas: the Complete Compendium*, MacMillan Publishing Co., Inc., New York, 1973.

deVegh, Geza and Mandi, Alber, *Craft of Ceramics*, D. Van Nostrand Co., Inc., Princeton, N.J. 1949.

D'Imperio, Dan, *The ABC's of Victorian Antiques*, Dodd, Mead and Co., New York, 1974.

Durant, Will, *Our Oriental Heritage*, Simon and Schuster, New York, 1954.

Hofsted, Jolyon, *Step-by-Step Ceramics*, Golden Press, New York, 1971.

Hone, Mikiso, *Japan, A Historical Survey*, Charles Scribner's Sons, New York, 1972.

Husfloen, Kyle, *Editorial*, The Antique Trader Weekly, Sept. 28, 1977.

Lehner, Ernest, *Symbols, Signs and Signets*, Dover Publishing Inc., New York city, 1969.

Lima, Paul and Candace, *The Enchantment of Hand Painted Nippon Porcelain*, Silverado Studios, Silverado, Calif., 1971.

Lord, Walter, *The Good Years*, Harper and Bros. Publishers, New York, 1960.

Matthews, Mary Lou, *American Kitchen Collectibles*, L-W Promotions, Gas City, Indiana, 1973.

Meyer, Florence C., *The Colorful World of Nippon*, Wallace Homestead Book Co., Des Moines, Iowa, 1971.

Hammond, Dorothy, *Confusing Collectibles*, Wallace-Homestead Book Co., Des Moines, Iowa, 1969.

Earle, Alice Morse, *China Collecting in America*, Charles Scribners Sons, New York, 1892.

Eation, Faith, *Dolls in Color*, Macmillan Publishing Co., New York, 1975.

Eberlein, Harold D. and Ramsdell, Roger W., *The Practical Book of Chinaware*, J.B. Lippincott Co., Philadelphia and New York, 1925.

Gorham, Hazel H., *Japanese and Oriental Ceramics*, Charles Tuttle Co., Rutland, Vt. and Tokyo, Japan, 1971.

Grant, Neil, *Victoria, Queen and Empress*, Franklin Watts, Inc., New York City, 1970.

Hall, John Whitney, *Japan from Prehistory to Modern Times*, Delacarte Press, New York, 1970.

Moffitt, R. & C. *Old Chinaware Summary, an Aid to Identification*, published by authors, Muncie, Indiana, 1960.

Moody, C.W., *Gouda Ceramics, The Art Nouveau Era of Holland*, published by author, 1970.

Moraini, Fosco, *Meeting with Japan*, The Viking Press, New York.

Morton, W. Scott, *Japan, Its History and Culture*, Thomas Y. Crowell Co., New York, 1970.

Nish, Ian *A Short History of Japan*, Frederick A. Prager Publisher, New York, 1968.

Peffer, Nathaniel, *The Far East*, The University of Michigan Press, 1958.

Peteln, Theodore A., *Oriental Motifs for Creative People*, Charles E. Tuttle Co., Rutland Vt. and Tokyo, Japan, 1965.

Pickard China and Glass, 1917 reprint catalog, Rainbow Publications, Costa Mesa, Calif., 1977.

Platt, Dorothy, Pickard, *The Story of Pickard China*, Everybody's Press Inc., Hanover, Pa., 1970.

Priolo, Joan B., *Ceramics and How to Decorate Them*, Bonanza Books, New York, 1958.

Ray, Marcia, *Collectible Ceramics*, Crown Publishers, Inc., New York, 1974.

Reischauer, Edwin O., *Japan: The Story of a Nation*, Alfred A. Knopf, Publisher, New York, 1970.

Rhodes, Daniel, *Clay and Glazes for the Potter*, Chilton Book Co., Radnor, Pa., 1957.

Robinson, Dorotha, *Nippon, Hand Painted China*, Forward's Color Productions, Manchester, Vt.

Rothenberg, Polly, *The Complete Book of Ceramic Art*, Crown Publishers, Inc., New york, 1972.

Rust, Gordon A., *Collector's Guide to Antique Porcelains*, Viking Press, New York, 1973.

Sandon, Henry, *Coffee Pots and Teapots for the Collector*, Arco Publishing Co., Inc., New York, 1977.

Schwartz, Marvin, D., and Wade, Betsy, *The New York Times Book of Antiques*, Quadrangle Books, New York City, 1972.

Sears, Roebuck & Co., 1908 Catalogue, reprint, edited by Joseph J. Schroeder, DBI Books, Inc., Northfield, Ill., 1971.

Seidensticker, Edward and the editors of Time-Life Books, *Life World Library, Japan*, Time & Life Books, New York, 1961.

Spencer, Cornelia, *Made in Japan*, Alfred A. Knopf, Inc., New York City, 1963.

Stitt, Irene, *Japanese Ceramics of the Last 100 Years*, Crown Publishers, New York, 1974.

Swann, Peter C., *An Introduction to the Arts of Japan*, Frederick A. Prager, Publisher, New York, 1958.

Tames, Richard, *Josiah Wedgwood*, Shire Publications Ltd., Aylesbury, England 1972.

The Best of Sears Collectibles 1905-1910, Arno Press, New York City, 1976.

The Society of International Cultural Relations Dolls Of Japan, printed for the International Exposition of Dolls in Antwerp, Nov. 1934, The Bunshoska Printing Co., Tokyo.

Tomlin, E., W., F., *Japan*, Walker and Co., New York 1973.

Trimble, Alberta C., *Modern Porcelain*, Harper and Bros., Publishers, New York, 1962.

Varley, H. Paul, *Japanese Culture*, Praeger Publishers, New York, 1973.

Walworth, Arthur, *Black Ships off Japan*, Archon Books, Hamden, Conn., 1966.

Williams, Barry, *Emerging Japan*, McGraw-Hill Book Co., New York, St. Louis, San Francisco, 1969.

Woodward, W., E., *The Way Our People Lived*, E.P. Dutton & Co., Inc., New York, 1944.